Come Walk With Me

ARE YOU WAITING FOR GOD
OR IS GOD WAITING FOR YOU?

JIM HOHNBERGER

Pacific Press® Publishing Association
Nampa, Idaho
Oshawa, Ontario, Canada
www.pacificpress.com

Cover design by Steve Lanto
Cover design resources from iStockphoto.com
Inside design by Aaron Troia
Inside photos and graphics provided by the author

To learn more about Jim Hohnberger and Empowered Living Ministries, visit www.empoweredlivingministries.org or call 1-877-755-8300. The author assumes full responsibility for the accuracy of all facts and quotations as cited in this book.

Unless otherwise noted, all Scriptures are quoted from The New King James Version, copyright © 1979, 1980, 1982, Thomas Nelson, Inc., Publishers.

Scripture quotations marked ASV are from the American Standard Version.

Scripture quotations marked KJV are from the King James Version.

Scripture quotation from *The Message*. Copyright © by Eugene H. Peterson, 1993, 1994, 1995, 1996, 2000, 2001, 2002. Used by permission of NavPress Publishing Group.

Scripture quotations marked NIV are from the HOLY BIBLE, NEW INTERNA-TIONAL VERSION®. Copyright © 1973, 1978, 1984 by International Bible Society. Used by permission of Zondervan Publishing House. All rights reserved.

Scripture quotations marked NLT are taken from the Holy Bible, New Living Translation, copyright © 1996, 2004. Used by permission of Tyndale House Publishers, Inc., Wheaton, Illinois 60189. All rights reserved.

Scriptures quoted from TEV are from the *Good News Bible*—Old Testament: Copyright © American Bible Society 1976, 1992; New Testament: Copyright © American Bible Society 1966, 1971, 1976, 1992.

You can obtain additional copies of this book by calling toll-free 1-800-765-6955 or by visiting http://www.adventistbookcenter.com.

Library of Congress Cataloging-in-Publication Data:

Hohnberger, Jim, 1948-
  Come, walk with me : are you waiting for God or is God waiting for
you? / Jim Hohnberger.
      p. cm.
  ISBN 13: 978-0-8163-2414-9 (hard cover)
  ISBN 10: 0-8163-2414-X
  1. Christian life—Seventh-day Adventist authors. I. Title.
  BV4501.3.H653 2010
  248.4'86732—dc22
                                                    2010018351

10 11 12 13 14 • 5 4 3 2 1

Dedication

If you are desperate for something more than religiosity;

if you are longing for the core of the gospel,

then this book is dedicated to you!

Acknowledgments

God sends us gifts in many ways. Understanding the need to enhance my writing and knowing my aversion to crossing *t*'s and dotting *i*'s, God gave me an outstanding personal assistant.

Jeanette Houghtelling, you made this book sing!

A Note to the Reader:

Every experience shared in this volume is true, although in a few cases, I have combined multiple individuals into a single character for the sake of brevity and clarity. In most cases, I have altered the names, locations, and other incidental characteristics to protect the privacy of the individuals involved. Any resemblance to person or persons besides my family and myself is strictly coincidental, except for those who have given me permission to use their names or stories.

Contents

Chapter 1

The Maze

O LORD, I know the way of man is not in himself;
It is not in man who walks to direct his own steps.

—Jeremiah 10:23

ather, let's get together!"

Even over the phone, I could sense Matthew's excitement. "Why?" I asked. "What's up?"

"We're going to go through a giant maze!"

"A what?"

"Yeah! A giant maze—a human maze. In West Glacier. It'll be a blast!"

"Who all is coming?"

"Angela and me, Andrew and Sarah, Janell, and you and Mother."

Matthew's excitement was contagious. I became excited too! I'd heard about human mazes, but had never gone through one. *This will be a breeze!* I thought. *Other people may have trouble figuring it out, but I'm quick-witted. I've got a nose for these things!*

As we drove up to the maze, I noticed a sign announcing the fastest time so far for completing it. Now, I don't know what goes through a female mind, but to a male mind, that's an instant challenge! My automatic response was, *I've got to match that time! I want to be number one! I can't wait to get into it!*

Throughout the maze there are platforms, so you can climb up and reorient yourself as needed. Before beginning our run, we surveyed the maze from one of those overlooks, and I noticed that my boys were studying the layout pretty carefully. Not me! I was eager to get started. I knew my internal compass would see me through. After all, I had earned a surveying minor in college. On top of that, I was very savvy in the woods. Drop me off anywhere, and I could find my way out. This would be a cinch!

Now I should stop here and say that I *assumed* our group would hang together. We are a close family—my two sons and their wives, my "adopted" daughter, and my wife—and I was their fearless leader. I was sure that they would be looking to me as the best "bird dog" and we would work out this maze together. Under my leadership, our collaborative wisdom would see us through.

So we entered the maze. Almost immediately, Matthew disappeared. Before I could figure out which direction he had gone, Janell took off down a different path. I was just drawing in a breath to tell them to wait up when Angela, Sarah, and Andrew chose their own routes, leaving Sally and me standing there all by ourselves. "Hey! Where are you all going?" I shouted. There was no answer. Well, at least Sally recognized my innate maze-conquering ability!

"I think we should go this way," I told her. "Follow me!" But to my dismay, naturally amiable Sally had her own opinion on the matter. Giggling, she headed off in a different direction, leaving me standing there all by myself! I was neither the leader of my clan nor of my queen!

I was stumped. This whole thing was not going according to plan—at least not according to *my* plan! How is a captain supposed to lead an army that deserts him? How could something that was supposed to be so much fun turn into such confusion so quickly? *Do they know something I don't?* I began to wonder. This was not funny; it was nerve-racking! I was frustrated.

So I started off in what I thought was the right direction—only to find myself ending up in a lot of dead ends. I could hear the voices of my family drawing farther and farther away. *They figured it out that quick? Why is everyone figuring it out except me? What's wrong with me?* The more I sensed their confidence, the more confused I became. And the more confused I became, the less confidence I had.

The embarrassing thing was that not only were my sons getting ahead of me, Janell was too. I started to become frantic. I *had* to figure it out! The thought occurred to me to sit down and let my emotions settle, but there was no way I could afford to let everyone get that much farther ahead of me. This maze thing wasn't turning out the way I had expected it to.

I climbed up on a platform and confirmed my fears. Most of my family was ahead of me, and my wife was not with me. This was not fun anymore. *Come on, Jim, get your act together,* I ordered myself. *Use your God-given gifts of common sense and direction and start moving!*

I looked ahead and tried to draw a mental map. *At the bottom of the steps, I turn right, then left, then right, then right again, then left . . .* I studied the maze a moment longer. *OK,* I told myself, *I've got it memorized.*

I ran down the stairs and turned right, then left. *Why doesn't that left turn seem to be the right direction? Oh no—another dead end!* I saw the steps to another platform and climbed up on it—only to recognize that it was the one I had just left! Talk about frustration!

Then the temptation hit. *Why not cheat? The bottoms of the fences are about a foot and a half off the ground. I could just crawl under the fences and get ahead. Then no one would know how desperate I feel.* I stood there toying with the impulse to take the easy way out.

But somehow, even in the midst of my frustration and panic, I didn't want to sink that low, so I tried something else. I called to the leaders of the pack. "Hey, Matthew, Janell, come up here. I want to team up with you."

The buddy system sounded really good to me right then. But they called back, "You're on your own, Father. We're ahead of you!"

On my own! I exclaimed to myself. *How can they do that to me?* This was getting serious! I started again, but kept running into blank walls, going around in circles, and ending up right back where I started.

Do you know what I said when I finally got out of that maze? I said, "I will never go in another one of those idiotic things again." I hated it! It made me feel so incompetent, so stupid! It was one of the worst "enjoyable" experiences I have ever had in my life. It was anything but fun. Everything about that maze offered the promise of delivery, while it was designed to be a dead end. Talk about frustration!

That's what the devil does in life too. He constructs mazes full of dead ends, dark corridors, and secret passages because he wants you to keep running in circles or throw in the towel. He wants to overwhelm you with discouragement, despair, and futility. He wants you to think, *Everyone's getting it, except me. Everyone's understanding it, except me.*

Most of us find ourselves too ashamed to admit that we're not getting it and too embarrassed to ask the questions that no one else is asking. We feel trapped in the maze of life and wonder where God is. We keep trying this direction and that, only to end up where we started. Let me share with you a few of my mazes in life.

The Catholic maze

I was eleven years old and in the fifth grade at Sacred Heart Catholic Grade School. All the other students seemed so much smarter than me. The teachers would ask questions, and other kids would raise their hands with the right answers. *How do they know all that?* I wondered. I felt so dumb!

When it was my turn to read to the class, I approached the front of the room with my head down, face burning in shame. You see, in second grade, an accident had knocked out my two front teeth. Unfortunately, they were my adult teeth. My dentist thought it best to try to save them and had fashioned a mold around them, hoping they would reset themselves. This made my upper lip protrude over my lower lip, and I spoke with a pronounced lisp. The kids called me "Icicle Mouth," "Bucky Beaver," and "Lispy." I could hear their snickers as I tried to get through my portion of the reading. Spelling bees were a nightmare for me because I was always on the losing side.

The playground wasn't a lot better. In fifth grade, the favorite games were basketball and dodgeball. I didn't play either very well, in part, because I didn't understand the rules or the strategy. But I was too bashful to ask someone to explain them to me. During a game, I was always wondering, *Who am I going to follow?*

I didn't fit in, so I pulled into myself. I wouldn't ask questions because that would make me feel even more stupid. The nun was a nice lady, but with so many kids to oversee, she didn't have much time to reach out to little Jimmy Hohnberger. I withdrew more and more and found myself to be very lonely.

I still remember the beginning of recess on one particular day. It was basketball that day, and the captains were choosing teams. You know how it goes. The captains take turns choosing from the would-be players until they each have five or six kids on their team. And I wasn't chosen; I was left out. Somehow not being picked was especially devastating to me on this day, so I resorted to the only source of help I could think of.

The school formed a wing on one side of the thousand-member church, with the playground located behind it. I walked all the way around the church to get to the door on the opposite side of the building. There was an entrance into the church from inside the school building, but I wouldn't go that way for fear of being questioned in the hallway. I timidly climbed the stone steps and slowly pushed open the tall oak door of the church. The cool, damp air of the large foyer sent a little chill into me. I peered inside and saw no one, so I stepped in. The lofty arches, enormous candelabras, and elaborate ornamentation made me feel very small and very insignificant.

As my eyes adjusted to the dim light, I saw the statue of Jesus Christ directly in front of me. I contemplated it briefly, but as a devout Catholic, I had been taught that you never approach God directly. A statue of Joseph was on my left, and one of Mary was on my right. I believed that Mary was the door to Jesus—that if I asked her to, she would intercede with Jesus to bless me. So I went over to Mary, put my dime in the little black box, and lit a candle. I can still see and smell the smoke as it wafted up toward Mary's blank stare. I didn't cry because I had been taught that men don't cry, but I was a broken little boy.

"Mary, please help me. Ask God to talk to me. I'm lonely and want direction. Please, Mary, talk to God for me. I want a friend. I want to fit in. I want to be smart and talented like the other kids."

I meant every word of my prayer. At that point in my life, fitting in was absolutely everything. "Please Mary, ask God to help me. Show me what to do. Direct me. Please work some miracle. I'm lonely. I don't fit in."

I stopped to listen for some kind of response. Once the echo of my quiet prayer died, there was nothing but silence—cold silence. No response. No answer. No help. I knew that I was sincere. I needed help. Why wouldn't Mary answer me?

Confessional

I decided that it must be my sins that were keeping Mary from answering my prayer. Oh boy! I knew what I had to do, but just the thought of it gave me sweaty palms. I hesitated, and then decided it was worth the risk. I just had to have help!

So I quietly, but deliberately, made my way down the dimly lit corridor to the little black booth known as the "confessional." My heart started pounding as I reached the curtained entrance. I knew the priest was in there because there was always one on duty. It felt so scary that I almost lost my nerve. What if he recognized me?

Gathering up my courage, I stepped into the confessional and took my place on the little wooden kneeler. After a few moments, the small door covering the window between the priest and me slid open. I still couldn't see him because a heavy screen remained between us. I hoped he could see as little of me as I could see of him.

"You have a confession to make?" The deep, rumbly voice made my heart beat even faster.

I cleared my throat and began, "Bless me, Father, for I have sinned. My last confession was a week ago."

There, I had done it! I had already told a lie! My sins were adding up before my confession had hardly even begun! You see, if I told him the truth—that I hadn't been to confession for more than two months—I knew I would have to do more penance. And right then, I wanted grace—not penance. If I got penance, instead of finding help, I'd only get more of what I had already gotten out on the playground. I couldn't handle that! So there I was, confessing my sins to a sinful man because I thought that was what was blocking God from helping me. And in the process, I was sinning further, because I was afraid of the consequences.

So I began to list my sins to the priest. "I sassed my mother twice. I disobeyed my father. And I stole some apples from my neighbor's apple tree."

There was an impressive pause, and then that deep voice rumbled again. "Your sins are forgiven."

Were they? I know now that they were not.[1]

"You must say one 'Our Father,' three 'Hail Marys,' and two 'Glory Bes,' " he continued.

"Yes, Father," I mumbled, relieved to have gotten off so easily. I left the confessional and returned to the statue of Mary. I said the prayers the priest had assigned me. Now, supposedly, there was no sin between God and me. I prayed again to Mary. Nothing happened. No help. Now I really felt that I was alone. *God isn't real,* I concluded. *He's not there for me. He might be there for others, but He's not there for me. I'm stupid—a sinner.* I couldn't figure it out.

The Mary syndrome

I now call this the "Mary syndrome"—accepting a substitute for the real thing. You may not have been raised a Catholic like me, but the Mary syndrome is ever present in the religions of today. They promise us God, but leave us short, dead-ended in legalism, conceptualism, churchianity, truthianity, missionanity—anything and everything as a substitute for the Living God who is there to personally guide us and empower us in our daily lives.

Instead, we join a church and become involved in outreach—programs, missions, Bible studies, and a whole host of activities that are good and have their place, but that can never supply the lack of God in the center of our experience.

I became an altar boy and assisted the priest in giving Mass—serving the holy Communion and the Eucharist. I thought that would earn me some favor with God. I was a good altar boy, but still there was nothing. No response. I couldn't get close to God.

I prayed to my favorite saint. Nothing.

I fasted, and on Fridays, we didn't eat meat. Nothing.

Every school day started with Mass. On the days I wasn't an altar boy, I

---

1. See Luke 5:21; 1 Timothy 2:5; Acts 10:43; 1 John 2:1.

always took my rosary and faithfully prayed my beads. Nothing. No response. Zilch. I can understand why Luther was so frustrated.

I partook of the Eucharist and thought, *This is supposed to be the actual body and blood of Jesus Christ!* When the priest placed the bread on my tongue, I always thought something would happen. I thought God would come into me and do something, but He didn't.

By the time I was old enough to make my own decisions, I was so fed up with dead-end religion that I wanted nothing more to do with it. I believed in God in a distant sort of way, but if He wouldn't speak to me or help me, I was no longer going to speak to Him. I wanted out! Out of this confusing, unending, futile maze. *I'm not playing this game,* I told myself. *It leaves me feeling stupid, alone, and empty.* Am I picking on the Catholic Church? No. I'm just relating my experience.

I fully and entirely abandoned that maze; not realizing that I was escaping one, only to throw myself into another. All I knew is that I wanted nothing more to do with the church. I wanted to make money, to become an important person, and to have fun. I was determined to "make it" in life.

The worldly maze

I started selling insurance. After a bit of a rocky start, I began doing very well. My company sent me to take advanced sales training. Part of this training was focused on decreasing the "lapse ratio." The lapse ratio is the number of policies that lapse during a given period compared to the total number of policies written at the beginning of that period. In other words, a lot of salesmen have great sign-up rates, but then their new clients switch to another company soon after signing up, and the company loses the profit.

Well, this training seminar included a meeting featuring the agents with the best lapse ratios. These agents went to the podium and talked about the things they credited for their success. Some sent out birthday cards to clients. Others sent Christmas cards. Still others thought refrigerator magnets and calendars worked really well.

When the last agent sat down, the master of ceremonies said, "Gentlemen, we have saved the best for last! The insurance agent with the lowest lapse ratio this year is—Jim Hohnberger!" [*Applause.*] "Jim, come forward and tell us how you do it!"

So I went forward and shared with the audience my secret of success. I hadn't done all the things others told me I was supposed to do. My formula was simple. I told my office staff, "Anyone who comes through this door with questions will get answers within twenty-four hours and will be treated with the utmost courtesy. You will greet them with a big, warm smile, and give them the best service anywhere." I always had an ear for my customers and held my clients.

I rose to the top 10 percent of agents in American Family Insurance. I was heralded as an icon for fulfillment. I got a lot of recognition. The company gave me awards—gold rings, diamond rings, and trips to Las Vegas and Hawaii. Everyone talked enthusiastically with me about how I set my goals, reached my goals, and how fulfilling it must be. But I was still empty. I smiled outwardly, but groaned inwardly. *Is this all there is?* I wondered. Of course, I never admitted that to anyone. I bragged about my accomplishments to my buddies and focused on getting a bigger home, bigger toys, and a bigger income.

I got into sports. *Keeping up with the Green Bay Packers is the thing, you know! Playing Monday-morning quarterback is so fulfilling. Swaggering around like a know-it-all will fool the other guys into thinking you've got it all together.* No one—and I mean no one—admits that this is only another dead-end corridor that promises escape while it is designed to frustrate you.

Then there was the hunting corridor. I went down that one big time. After all, if you know how to shoot a gun and kill a large animal, you must be powerful! You must be a real man! You must have everything under control! At least that's the façade everyone puts on.

Different things become your gods in different mazes, but you never find the way out. You're left empty and deteriorating—but you keep it to yourself. You're trained to believe that whatever corridor you're in, it has the greatest thing in the world, whether it's the Green Bay Packers, rock climbing, making money, or anything else you might get into. No one ever tells you that it doesn't work, and you don't admit to anyone else that it's not working for you because that's not acceptable.

Sally and I got into the party life. We wanted to have fun! What we found out is that the party life is scary. I remember a drinking party down in our basement with our neighbors and friends. We were playing music and dancing. Someone brought out the game Twister. Now that's a fairly harmless game when you're playing with your kids, but not when you're playing it with someone else's wife!

Late in the evening, I had to go upstairs to use the bathroom. While I was in there, the neighbor's wife came into the bathroom and pressed up against me. I left the bathroom. That kind of thing just wasn't in me. All I got out of that night was a headache in the morning.

But, hey, we had a great time, right? We were in search of the god of fun, joy, and prosperity, but we couldn't find him because someone else always had more fun, joy, or money than we did. In the process, Sally and I grew distant from each other. We found no inner peace.

Another corridor we followed in the worldly maze was a book club. You signed up and paid a monthly subscription, and then you regularly received the book of the month. Three of the books we received were on witchcraft. Black magic really intrigued me—not for spiritual reasons; it was more out of curiosity. I was fascinated with mysterious things. I didn't take God seriously, neither did I believe the devil was much of a threat.

Devil's food cake

We started experimenting with some of the black magic stuff during our drinking parties. We learned how to make our dining room table dance. It was fun. I didn't think it was anything to be afraid of. We thought it was an adventure into a science that we didn't understand.

The next step was to get a Ouija board. About this time, we started studying the Bible with Protestants. One night we had a drinking party. I had the Ouija board out and was playing with it. While everyone was watching, I asked it the question "What's my favorite cake?"

The board started jiggling around and then moved very decisively to spell out DEVIL'S FOOD CAKE. I got an eerie feeling, and everyone started laughing. "OK, Jim. You're doing it. How'd you do that?"

"I didn't do it," I insisted. "No one touched that board!"

"Oh, come on, Jim. You must have some trick that made it spell out those words."

But I didn't. Some invisible force had moved the pointer to those letters in perfect order. I began wondering if I was dealing with something more than I had reckoned with.

I know now that I was involved in a very serious game. The devil was trying to keep me running in one maze after another, and he wants the same for you too. He doesn't care which maze we're in, as long as we stay in it. He's even willing to give us profound spiritual experiences that lead us to believe we're finding God—as long as we never connect with the God of the Bible.

On the other hand, God is always seeking an avenue to draw us to Himself, to place us on the "Highway of Holiness"[2] where we are safe from the designs of the devil.

As Sally and I began studying the Bible, God was moving upon our hearts, but the devil wanted to intimidate us. I went through a three-month period of waking up at night feeling the devil's hands on my neck, choking me. I would be sweating profusely and terrified to get out of bed. The attacks were exhausting, and I didn't know what to do about them.

---

2. Isaiah 35:8.

The crisis came one evening about seven-thirty. We lived on Peach Tree Lane at that time, in a modern home with a sunken living room. On one side of the living room was a massive fireplace with a mantel above it and tall bookcases on either side. Sally was taking a shower, and I was sitting across from the fireplace, reading the Bible. My eyes wandered from the pages of the Bible and rested on those books of witchcraft lying on a shelf just to the right of the fireplace and above the mantel. A thought came to me, urging, *"Burn those books!"* At the same time, I felt a cold, sinister presence enter the room and press itself upon me—the same presence I felt at night when I was being choked. I sat riveted in my chair, terrified of what might happen if I stood up. Finally, I forced myself to stand and walk over to the mantel—feeling that at any moment I would be knocked off my feet. I picked up the witchcraft books. Tearing off the covers and ripping them up as much as I could, I threw them into the fire. As I did so, the oppressive presence left, and I never had encounters with the devil again. Since then, I've often wondered how many Christians have given the devil access to their homes through the books, music, magazines, and videos they possess.

The Protestant maze

Sally and I were introduced to the Bible through Protestantism. I said, "This is truth. This is it!" I threw myself into the truth and into the understanding of the truth and the sharing of the truth. We had discovered a lamp for our feet and a light for our path.[3] This was what we had been missing all our lives. We left the worldly maze and joined a Protestant church by baptism. No one told us that we were entering yet another maze.

The first dead end I found was theological truth. Yes, I believe that the Bible is the inerrant Word of God and that it is the acid test of my creed. However, knowledge of the truth *alone* can leave me no better off than I was when I was in the clutches of the devil himself. Those rays of light that so warmed my heart at first, in time, threatened to lock me in greater darkness than I had known before.

How can that be? you ask.

It can happen because when we substitute the *rays* of light for the *Source* of light, they soon become dark. And when we substitute the truth for God Himself, truth becomes no more effective in our lives than the statue of Mary was to me as an eleven-year-old boy.[4]

I was led to believe that the truth was an end in and of itself. I began to base

---

3. See Psalm 119:115.
4. See John 5:39.

my security on my ability to understand the truth, to master the truth, to explain it to others, and to defend it before others. I came to believe that if I possessed all the truth for the last days, then I was the "enlightened one"—a Christian. But was I? The devil understands the truth better than any of us; but does that make him a Christian? I don't think so! So there has to be more to the picture than mere superior theological knowledge.

The second dead end—lifestyle and reforms—led to a sad experience as well. I became a vegetarian. I left off alcohol, tobacco, caffeinated drinks, ungodly entertainment, worldly music and dress, swearing, off-color jokes, and of course, I began to faithfully return my tithes and give offerings. I was sure looking a lot better than before, and I *was* better off in many ways. But a subtle danger entered. I started to feel like Saul did before he became the apostle Paul: "Concerning the righteousness which is in the law, blameless."[5] Pride in the accomplishments of my strong will distorted my perception of myself, and I felt that now I was spiritually rich and in need of nothing else.[6]

The church Sally and I fellowshiped with told us that our intellectual assent to doctrinal truth and the conformity of our lifestyle to proper Christian values proved that we had been "born again." We were baptized into the church. We were sincere and had surrendered to the accepted norms of fellow believers; that much was true. But we were led to believe that we were now complete and had only one corridor left to follow. I threw myself into it with all the vigor I possessed.

That third dead-end corridor was outreach—evangelism and giving Bible studies. I honestly believed that if I converted others to the same doctrines and lifestyle that I had subscribed to, I would be following all that was involved in the gospel commission to "go . . . and make disciples of all the nations."[7]

The talents I had developed in sales made me an able promoter and a zealous defender of the faith. Soon more than a dozen people were baptized into my church. I was seen as a champion of truth and was heralded for my success. The pats on the back reminded me a bit too much of my insurance company's response to my good sales record. I became somewhat proud of my accomplishments and lifted up myself, my truth, and my church to others.

I didn't know it then, but this was one of the most dangerous periods of my life. Why? Because I was so close to the genuine path that I didn't recognize that the devil had shunted me—ever so slightly—onto a different path, a path that connected me with the church rather than with God. Those two paths

---

5. Philippians 3:6.
6. Revelation 3:17.
7. Matthew 28:19.

traveled along together as far as my eye could see, but God knew where this counterfeit path would lead. He knew it would lead me to the very same place it had led the Jews in Christ's day. They fiercely defended their theological truth while crucifying the One who is the Truth. Their churchianity had become impotent. It existed, not for the benefit of its members or for the honor of the God of the universe, but for its own sake. Today's Christian church is facing a similar crisis.

As time went on, I found myself going through the same busy round of activities that had characterized life in the worldly maze, and a familiar, but unwelcome emptiness began to nag at me. It's scary! To come so close and to think that you have found it and to feel that what you have found is good—yet not to be delivered and not find fulfillment and not know why! I had found it, that was true, but I was still empty.

I said to myself, *Haven't I been here before? Have I just gone in another circle? Is there no way out of this dilemma? Why am I back to this sense of emptiness again? These last few corridors seemed to offer so much.*

I had to get a handle on the bigger picture. So I climbed up onto the platform of my mind's overlook to think things through. Why was I so empty behind closed doors? I had no power over my anger, irritation, and hot temper. I felt lonely and disconnected—pulled in a thousand different directions, trying to meet a thousand different expectations. I could never do enough to arrive at any sense of fulfillment and peace. My relationship with Sally had become stale and distant. In my presence, my sons obeyed for fear of my quick reprisals, but behind my back, they did their own thing. And I realized that I didn't really know them. It all seemed so futile.

I looked at those who had been in this maze longer than I had. I saw many unhappy people with broken relationships and discontented dispositions, running the round of religion and putting on façades to cover up the dysfunction of their lives.

Some families shouted and screamed and called each other names, but never resolved their differences. Others never fought, but they were isolated in the dark cave of depression and never worked past their difficulties. Some people went around like porcupines; they were fine as long as you stroked them the right way, but as soon as you didn't, they sent sharp quills into your tender flesh. Others I met had no power over their appetites or sexual impulses.

The frequency of divorce in the church was just a little behind that in the world. Rebellion in the youth was considered normal. I read 2 Timothy 3:2–4 and felt that the description there fit the lives of God's professed people behind closed doors all too well—lovers of selves who had a form of godliness, but no power to transform their characters or to heal their relationships. *Is this what I want for my family or myself?* I asked myself.

I looked around again. Surely the pastors and the congregational leaders had it figured out. They appeared to be far ahead of me in this maze. I asked them to help me, but they confessed they were in the same jam I was in. They had nothing to offer me other than to keep doing what I was doing. I was reminded of the old definition of insanity—to keep doing the same thing over and over again while expecting a different result.

Is this all there is? I agonized. *Is life really meant to be nothing more than empty circles and discouraging dead ends? Am I missing something? It seems we're all like cars without engines, lightbulbs without electricity, bodies without breath. The equipment is good, but where's the vital power?*

In the midst of my disillusionment, I heard Someone calling my name.[8] I turned and saw that the call came from a short gate, leading to a narrow corridor right next to the one I had just been following.[9] The gate was dusty from disuse, and I didn't know much about it. But the Voice kept calling, *"Open this door, Jim. 'You search the Scriptures, for in them you think you have eternal life; and these are they which testify of Me.'*[10] *'Come to Me.'*[11] *I will give you an abundant life in the place of your empty existence.*[12] *Take My hand,*[13] *and I'll lead you safely through the mazes of religion and this world.*[14] *You will never be alone.*[15] *I will empower you where you are weak,*[16] *instruct you where you are ignorant,*[17] *and balance you where you are imbalanced.*[18] *I will help you bring that spark of first love back into your marriage*[19] *and show you how to win the hearts of your sons.*[20] *Come—walk with Me."*[21]

I hesitated, weighing the narrowness and disuse of that gate against the assurance of the One who was inviting me through it. "I'd like to step through it, Lord. What You're offering me is everything I've been looking for—but I'm not sure I can fit through there. You see, I've got this pack on my back

---

8. See Revelation 3:20; Isaiah 43:1.
9. See Matthew 7:14.
10. John 5:39.
11. Matthew 11:28.
12. See John 10:10; 4:14; Psalm 36:9; Jeremiah 2:13.
13. See Isaiah 41:13.
14. See John 10:4; Psalm 32:8; Isaiah 30:21.
15. See Hebrews 13:5.
16. See Titus 2:11–14; 2 Peter 1:3, 4.
17. See James 1:5.
18. See Hebrews 12:5–11.
19. See Ephesians 5:25–31.
20. See Ephesians 6:4; Malachi 4:6.
21. See Genesis 5:24; 6:9; Matthew 11:28–30.

that I've carried all my life. I don't think I can get through the door with it on."

"*You're right, Jim. You are carrying around a big bundle of preeminence. You are the lord of your own life, and you think that you're sufficient and qualified to run it. You'll have to leave that bundle behind to walk through this door. You can no longer be the center of your life. I must be! I must have preeminence in all things.*"[22]

Questions to ponder or discuss with others:

1. Do you feel trapped in the maze of life and wonder where God is?
2. Are you involved in the "Mary syndrome" (substituting something in the place of God), leaving you to feel short, empty, and dead-ended?
3. Are you fed up with dead-end religion?
4. Has the worldly maze (a bigger home, bigger toys, or a bigger income) left you empty?
5. Are you chasing after the god of fun, joy, sports, and prosperity?
6. Have you given the devil access to your home through the books, music, magazines, and videos you possess?
7. Are you running into dead ends in the Protestant maze?
8. Has your "churchianity" rendered you impotent in your daily life behind closed doors?
9. Have you found power over your anger, irritation, appetite, emotions, eyes, sexual passions, tongue, and pride?
10. Are you missing something deep down?

---

22. Colossians 1:18; Deuteronomy 6:5.

Chapter 2

The Issue

That in all things He may have the preeminence.

—Colossians 1:18

Sweat streamed down my face and neck and soaked my shirt as I laboriously trudged up the mountain. The pack on my back seemed to grow heavier with each step, but I knew I couldn't do without it. It was my means of survival. I had to have my tent and sleeping bag, my food and water, and my extra layers of warm clothing.

Being self-sufficient in the wilderness—that's one thing I love about backpacking. Yet my very self-sufficiency was exhausting me.

I thought about John Muir, the famous naturalist and mountaineer. He would roll up "some bread and tea in a pair of blankets with some sugar and a tin cup and set off" for months.[1] He was footloose and fancy-free. No heavy pack to weigh him down! He, and other men like him, knew how to be sustained by what the Creator has already provided in nature. I was a bit envious of their freedom, but then I had

---

1. John Parker Huber, "John Muir's Menu," John Muir Exhibit, http://www.sierraclub.org/john_muir_exhibit/frameindex.html?http://www.sierraclub.org/JOHN_MUIR_EXHIBIT/life/john_muir_menu_j_parker_huber.html.

the thought of being up here without my tent or sleeping bag—*Brrr*! And the thought of exchanging my hash browns and pancakes for plain bread or berries—well, I thought I'd keep my pack! It seemed a bit scary to take that step away from predictable comfort into the unknown—even though the freedom was inviting.

All of us carry around a pack of preeminence. As children of a fallen race, we figure out pretty early in life that we want to run our own lives. We develop ways to be in charge, to take care of ourselves, to avoid being uncomfortable or getting hurt. We become independent. We rely on our own resources to manage life and have our needs met. Once in a while we run into someone or hear of someone, such as Abraham, Paul, or Martin Luther, who has left the pack behind. We envy his or her freedom, but the thought of what it would cost to follow in his or her footsteps seems too great a price to pay. So we labor on, climbing the mountains of life, sweating and straining, burdened by the heavy pack on our back, yet fearfully dependent upon it.

Different people carry different things in their backpacks, but every pack has one thing in common—the attempt to live life on our own terms. As a national fast-food franchise puts it, "Have it your way!"

So what's in your pack? Where do you see yourself in the following scenarios?

The root issue

It was lunchtime in the conference cafeteria at one of our annual ministry seminars. Most of us had finished eating, but we lingered at the tables, enjoying the remnants of our pleasant conversation. Out of the corner of my eye, I noticed Betty, a sweet girl in her midtwenties, moving from table to table, picking up people's trays and carrying them to the kitchen. I had known Betty and her family for years. She was a devoted, religious girl who loved the Scriptures and her church. Whenever a spiritual meeting was taking place, you could count on Betty to be there with her smile and her support.

I watched her a little closer. As Betty picked up each tray, the person she was serving got a pleased, surprised expression on his or her face and then remarked about what a lovely young lady she was. Betty would smile shyly, blush a little, and move on.

That evening at supper, I noticed the same thing happening. When Betty came to pick up my tray, I thanked her and then asked, "Betty, why do you help so many people with their trays?"

She looked at me a bit puzzled, cocked her head to one side, and replied, "Oh, I like to serve!"

"That's really sweet, Betty. Thank you for being so thoughtful," I commented and stood up to leave the dining hall.

Later that evening, I was headed to my cabin when Betty called to me across the field, "Mr. Hohnberger, can you wait a minute? I'd like to talk to you."

When she reached me, I noticed she looked troubled. "What's on your mind, Betty?"

She hesitated, studying her toes, then looked up at me. "I don't exactly know why, Mr. Hohnberger, but your question at supper has kept coming back to my mind. It bothered me all through the evening meeting. Finally, during the closing prayer, I realized why."

She glanced up just long enough so that I could see tears in her eyes.

"Why? What do you mean?" I asked gently.

Gathering her courage and looking me in the eye, she replied, "I think there is a deeper motivation in my desire to serve people—a motivation that I wasn't really in touch with. I think I like people to see me as a Christian, and I really enjoy their kind words."

"In other words, you are really doing it for yourself?"

"Uh . . . I guess I am. It fills an emptiness in me."

That was the beginning of a very deep conversation between the two of us about what really rules us. This young lady was raised in an overly controlling environment that hindered her from thinking for herself and making her own decisions. She learned that seeking the approval of others meant emotional survival. It had become a way of life for her. At all costs, she avoided conflict with those she respected; she served others to win their positive strokes. The approval of others was her pack of preeminence.

Now I'm not saying that it's wrong to serve others or that it's un-Christian to enjoy their genuine appreciation. But we must ask ourselves which spirit is leading us. Is it a spirit of self-exaltation, a spirit that seeks the approval of others? Or are we interested primarily in the approval of God? There is a big difference! When we begin to build our lives around the approval of others, we are seeking life on our own terms, and we wind up with an empty existence that only temporarily satisfies, rather than an abundant life. It seems that we can have the "forms" of religion in place; but if we are ultimately the ones in charge, then—perhaps even unknown to us—we carry with us the root problem that got us all in trouble in the first place.

This spirit of self-exaltation can show up anywhere: at home, at school, at work, and even at church.

Why do we do what we do?

It was church nominating committee time, and new church officers were being selected. I noticed Chris was being extra friendly to the people at church.

Chris attends church on a regular basis and helps teach the morning Bible study class. He loves to be involved in discussions on biblical topics and is an expert when it comes to playing the devil's advocate. When he made his way over to me that morning, I wondered what was on his mind. After exchanging the usual polite formalities, he stepped a little closer and asked in a confidential tone of voice, "Jim, do you have any concerns about how the church is being operated right now? Do you feel that your issues are being heard?"

"Why do you ask?"

"Well, I just want you to know that I feel called to the position of elder this year; and if I'm voted in as an elder, I will be a voice for the people. If you have any problems, come to me, and I'll make sure your concerns are addressed properly."

Chris appeared more congenial and accommodating than I had ever known him to be, so I wondered, *Is Chris truly responding to God's call to this position or is he lobbying for himself?* I didn't know, but soon afterwards, he was voted to be an elder, and I made a mental note of his promise to me.

Some time later, while worshiping at church, the special music for the day troubled me. I know that music is a very sensitive issue and one that is likely to rile the saints. However, I am very concerned when I see the same style of music that I used to enjoy in nightclubs be presented in church. I don't believe that music is morally neutral; I believe we have an obligation to guard the sacredness of the worship service. As I prayerfully considered the situation, I decided to share my viewpoint with Chris.

Stepping aside with him, I presented my perspective. He was warm at first, but when he started to realize the nature of my concern, his face darkened. He abruptly interrupted me, saying, "Look, Jim, that special music was a real blessing to me, and if you don't like it, it is your responsibility to go talk to the musicians yourself. But, be warned! They are pretty sensitive to criticism." With that, he turned and walked away.

Wow! What happened to his promise to consider any concerns I might have? I decided it must have been mere campaign rhetoric. It seemed to me that his service to the church was really more for himself and his own image than it was for his church and his God. Can self-interest motivate our handling of church offices and duties? I'm afraid so. In fact, I've had to take stock of that in my own experience.

Being "somebody"

After joining a Protestant church, I became very zealous for the truth that I had learned. At my office, I displayed a rack of various Bible-study brochures. When someone was leaving my office, I would invite them to look over the topics presented and pick out anything that interested them. Some clients would come back to me with questions. Then I'd offer to come to their homes in the evenings and answer their questions using my Bible and concordance. This led to a weekly Bible study.

Soon baptisms started flowing into the local church. About every six months, a new couple would be baptized. This went on for more than three years. The church was impressed. "Jim Hohnberger is a very spiritual man!" members remarked.

But over time, a troubling pattern emerged. Most of "my" converts started having problems, and sooner or later, they would stop attending the church. I couldn't figure out what the problem was. I know now, but I didn't then. As Romans 10:2, 3 says, I had "a zeal for God, but not according to knowledge." I was "ignorant of God's righteousness" and went about "seeking to establish [my] own righteousness." That righteousness was found in converting people to the facts of my faith and connecting them to my church. I gave them what I had. But what I had was a deficient gospel. As I look back, I believe what I did was more for me and my church than it was for these new members and God.

The motive for our evangelism is very important. Are we really interested in those to whom we witness? Or are we interested in them for ourselves? I've had to do some serious introspection on this question.

To my knowledge, only one person who was baptized through my Bible studies still remains in the church today. It's not that what I gave them was wrong. It's that it wasn't centered on God nor was it done for the love of Jesus.

The bottom-line question is this: What were my true motivations for what I did? I can honestly say that I wanted to be somebody important. I had grown up feeling like a nobody, and that didn't feel very comfortable. I intuitively thought that being "somebody" would insulate me from the feelings of loneliness and inadequacy that had so plagued my school days. Thus even my evangelism was fraught with the root problem—that bundle of preeminence.

I am not alone in this experience. I have been in church lobbies where soulwinning achievement plaques were proudly displayed. Tell me, how would you feel if you had been invited to a Bible study or an evangelistic sermon and you saw these kinds of plaques on the wall? I don't know about you, but I would wonder if the people who had invited me were genuinely interested in helping me or whether they were on a trophy hunt. In our witnessing, are we truly seeking to benefit people, with nothing in it for us?

This is hard stuff! Most of us don't like to face the searching question, Why do I do what I do? We'd rather just do it. Probing deep into our own hearts is likely to turn up uncomfortable answers that we either don't know what to do with or don't want to face. It may stir up feelings of guilt or shame. Please don't misunderstand me. This kind of introspection is not for the purpose of dumping a load of guilt on either you or me. It's to help us get to the real reason we wander in our various mazes and wind up empty.

The key issue

The rich young ruler felt that emptiness. He was zealous in his religious duties, yet he had this nagging sense that something was missing. When Jesus pointed out that he needed to keep God's commandments, he could sincerely reply that he had kept them all from his youth. He didn't think he was missing anything. And yet—what could it be? Like so many of us, he had a hard time coming to terms with that pack of preeminence. It seems so right, so justifiable, so much a part of us that we don't realize it doesn't belong on our backs. God knows how to put His finger right on the root issue. That's why Jesus said to the rich young ruler, "One thing you lack: Go your way, sell whatever you have and give to the poor, and you will have treasure in heaven; and come, take up the cross, and follow Me."[2] It's not that wealth is evil in and of itself. God blessed both Abraham and Job with great wealth. But there is a deeper issue at hand. Jesus knew that young man placed his dependence in his financial portfolio. Selfishness ruled his inner motivations; and selfishness is our attempt to live life on our own terms, to control everyone and everything around us for the purpose of preserving ourselves.

Jesus offered that young man the way out of the empty mazes of life. He said, "Take off that pack of preeminence. I will provide for you as you go." Sadly, like many in our day, that young man did not recognize the value of what he was being offered. Like me and my wilderness backpack, to exchange security and comfort for real freedom seemed too high a price to pay. He turned sadly back to his mazes, clinging tightly to his pack of preeminence.

Scripture doesn't tell us what happened to that young man down the road, but I can guess, because I've seen it played out in my generation all too many times.

Allen was a good friend who was a wizard at the nursing home business. I mean, he was brilliant when it came to developing his chain of long-term care facilities. He had started as the administrator of a nursing home and eventually worked his way up to becoming the owner of the nursing home. Then he began leveraging his finances to build a chain of facilities covering several states.

Allen was not what I would call an overly religious man. He attended church mainly at Christmas, Easter, and for weddings he couldn't avoid. How-

---

2. Mark 10:21.

ever, he was very active on the church board—a position he managed to secure with his large donations. He liked that position of influence because he felt he could make a difference. When some person or some company was in trouble, he liked to come to the rescue. He loved to turn bad situations around. He was the guy that always ended up wearing the white hat.

Over the years, when we talked, Allen would tell me of the long hours he was putting into growing his business and enlarging his influence. He worked from early morning until late at night. I asked him how this was affecting his health, his marriage, and his children. (Of course, when you're young, you think you're invincible, and you tend to take your health for granted.)

"Jim, I don't know what is wrong with Edith. I mean, I work these long hours so I can make her happy," Allen confided.

"Really, Allen? Is that what makes her happy?"

"Well, it should. She has all the money she could possibly want. I built her a fantastic new home last year on lakefront property and furnished it with anything she wanted. She has a new sports car, wears designer clothes, and has maids to keep her house. She is a lady of leisure. Why is she always complaining? And the kids—they drive me nuts! 'Daddy, Daddy! Won't you play with me? Won't you read me a story? Won't you go for a bike ride with me?' Can't they be satisfied? They have all the latest toys and doodads that any kid could want. I tell you, Jim, that if I have to listen to my wife and kids complain like they do, I'd just rather work."

"But, Allen, did Edith marry you for your money? You weren't wealthy when you got married, were you? Maybe she doesn't want all that stuff as much as she wants you. And your kids; they grow up so fast. They need your companionship far more than they need all the stuff you're giving them. What are you sacrificing for all this wealth and success?"

We talked at length, and Allen began to see that his prosperity was robbing him of life's real treasures. But, like the rich young ruler, he just couldn't bring himself to let it go and refocus his life.

In time, his assets added up to more than thirty-five million dollars. Unfortunately, he had leveraged his assets based on a very optimistic view of the economy, and when the economic downturn began, he found himself in deep trouble. As the value of his holdings declined with the downward spiraling economy, his debts became insurmountable, and he faced bankruptcy.

His wife was on the verge of divorcing him; his kids, now in their late teens, wanted nothing to do with him, while at the same time expecting a free flow of cash. His doctor had given him serious warnings about his heart condition, and he was losing his businesses. He faced not only financial bankruptcy, but also spiritual, physical, and relational disaster.

That's what holding on to this pack of preeminence eventually winds up doing to us. Instead of sustaining us, it crushes us; or at best, it fails us when we most need it.

So let's ask ourselves some difficult questions. What is our motive in business? Why do we hold a church office? Why do we preach? What drives us in friendship or marriage or parenting? What is our motive when we discipline our children (or avoid disciplining them)? Is it truly for their long-term benefit or is it for our short-term relief? Do we want them to appear like good soldiers, all in a row, so that we look good? Or maybe we just want them out of our hair.

What drives us to excel in athletics or music? As a young woman, my personal assistant dreamed of being a concert pianist. She had a true love for music, but underlying that love was the sense that being accomplished and well-known would give her significance in the place of her relational disconnectedness. It wasn't that her dream was bad, but the motivation behind her dream was her pack of preeminence. What fuels your dreams? What do you depend on, invest in, and build your life around?

"In the know"

I was just stepping down from the platform after one of my meetings when Bill approached me. "Jim, I've got to talk to you," Bill began hurriedly. "The other day, my wife threatened to take a sledgehammer to my computer."

"Really! Why?"

"I have no idea! I was just checking my e-mail and catching up on the headlines. Where I work, you've got to know what's going on or you look like a real dummy."

Bill was a bookish sort of guy. He wore thick glasses, had a pen tucked above his ear, and had a spare tire around his middle. I noticed that his Bible was dog-eared, falling apart, and stuffed with odds and ends of papers and notes. His story unfolded something like this.

It had been a long day on the job. Bill was sitting at his computer, checking his e-mail and scoping out the news. Images of Jerry kept floating in and out of his mind. Jerry always seemed to know everything that was going on—whether it was the president's most recent foreign policy conference or the latest sporting event. It really irked Bill that Jerry was such a know-it-all. But at the same time, he wanted to be in the know too.

Bill scanned the headlines and clicked on the stories that seemed the most unusual or significant. Soon he was fully engrossed. He didn't know how much time had gone by, but he became vaguely aware that his five-year-old daughter was standing beside him, tugging on his sleeve.

When he glanced in her direction, she asked hopefully, "Daddy, I have all my dollies dressed for bed, and I need a Daddy to tuck them in. Will you play house with me? Just for a little bit?"

Bill frowned and let out a deep sigh. "Betsy, honey, can't you see that Daddy is busy? You just pretend to be the Mommy and tuck your dollies in bed yourself."

If Bill had been paying attention, he would have seen Betsy's shoulders slump and her eyes drop as she stood there a moment longer, hoping Daddy would change his mind. But Bill was too busy trying to mentally grapple with an item about the latest proposal for a national health care program to notice. This was important stuff!

His eight-year-old son didn't understand that when he came charging through the back door. "Hey, Dad, come quick! There's a red-tailed hawk circling low over the back field. Blackie is out there, and I think the hawk might be after her. Come quick!"

"Huh?" grunted Bill. By now he had moved on to the NFL Web site and was sorting through the latest stats on which teams had the best chance for making it to the Super Bowl. "Oh, don't worry, Jimmy. Blackie is a smart cat; she'll be just fine."

"But, Dad, what if she isn't? Please come!" Jimmy sounded desperate. Blackie was an older, but much beloved pet cat that Jimmy had grown up with.

Turning to look at him, Bill barked, "Look, Jimmy. I'm in the middle of something important. Don't worry about it. I'm not coming right now. Let Blackie be a cat and fend for herself!"

Jimmy's big blue eyes filled with tears, but he turned and ran back out the door to do what he could for Blackie. Bill hardly noticed. He was already immersed again in the world of quarterbacks and touchdowns.

The entire evening passed, and Bill still sat transfixed before his computer monitor. The sounds of his wife cleaning up the dinner dishes, helping the children get their baths, and tucking them in bed were only so much background noise.

She came in a little later. "Honey, can I talk to you about something that's been on my mind all day?"

"Later, sweetheart, later."

A few moments later, Bill was shocked out of his virtual reverie by a sudden movement at his side. His usually gentle wife stood there with indignant eyes and a raised sledgehammer. "Bill, I've had enough of that thing! Night after night, you sit glued to that screen. When are you going to come back to earth?"

So what's driving Bill? Does being "in the know" really amount to that much? Why is it so important to avoid looking like a dummy at work? Isn't religion supposed to teach the Bills in its midst to be in tune with the voice of their conscience instead of leaving them as the one running the show?

A false sense of belonging

Joan is a young lady who seems to have it together. She is organized, talented, multiskilled, intelligent, outgoing, and spiritual. She eats right, dresses attractively and modestly, and is honest, thoughtful, and kind. She loves her church and has started a ministry that shares books with those unable to purchase them for themselves. She's a person you almost can't help but like. As we visited one day, she told me about a new aspect to her life that she was finding quite fascinating—Facebook. Here's one of her typical mornings.

She cuddles up in her favorite rocker with her laptop computer. Glancing at the clock, she tells herself, *I'll give myself just fifteen minutes, and then I've got to get into my exercise program. Seems like I've missed it a lot lately. And speaking of missing things—I wonder if I have anything left to wear. I haven't done the laundry for a long time.* Glancing over her living room, she sighs. *Guess I'll have to get out the vacuum cleaner and the dust rag and tidy up some of this clutter one of these days too.*

A little nagging thought whispers in her mind, *Why not do it now? You could get a good start toward putting things in order in just fifteen minutes. Facebook can wait.* She ponders the idea a moment and then opens her laptop. She just has to see what is going on there.

The first thing she notices is three new friend requests. She scans their pictures and names. Only one of them is a personal acquaintance. The others are friends of a friend. She quickly clicks on the links to confirm them as friends and smiles to herself. *That brings my total number of friends up to 389. It's fun to see how many I can collect!* She then clicks on the picture of the first one, looks at the information, and glances through the pictures. Then she notices the list of this person's friends. Scrolling through the list, one face jumps out at her. It's Larry, her old boyfriend. *That scamp,* she thinks. *I wonder what he's up to now. I hope he's not too happy. Let me see what kind of information I can find out about him.* After poking around a little, she is pleased to discover that Larry has been plagued with some hard times.

Smiling smugly to herself, she goes back to her own page and reads through all the new posts, clicking on some of the links and sending brief messages to various ones. It is all rather absorbing, and when she looks up again, an hour and fifteen minutes has gone by. She jumps up. *Oh boy, I'd better hurry or I'm going to be late to work again. How did the time slip by so quickly? So much for exercising or cleaning today. Tomorrow, I'll have to do that first.*

Can you relate to Joan? She thinks she has 389 friends, but does she really? As we talked, Joan realized that few of these "friendships" have any depth or substance. Most of them are bogus friendships that lead her to lean on a false sense of belonging. It's very easy to avoid the risks of real relationship in the virtual world. One can present just about any image they care to and hide what they don't want seen. On the other hand, others can learn a lot about you without having to make any investment in a relationship with you.

Now, don't get me wrong. There is a proper place for computers, e-mail, and perhaps, for some, even social networks. But we've got to be honest with ourselves about our motivation for being involved in these things and the impact they are having on our lives. Do we rule them or do they own us? If they own us, then aren't they our masters? And aren't we supposed to have only one Master?

Power play

More than twenty-five years ago, Sally and I moved to the wilderness of northwestern Montana where we live fifty miles from the nearest power and phone lines. So we've been off the grid for a long time. We heat and cook with wood, have a propane refrigerator, and rely on our propane-fueled generator and a bank of batteries to supply our electrical needs. A few years ago, we invested in a set of solar panels to supplement our generator's power production.

To my delight, the solar panels are able to supply nearly 100 percent of our energy needs—from April to October. November through March are cloudier months, and the sun passes through the sky at a more southern angle, so the panels supply only about 50 percent of what we need. Of course, the power system is my little baby, and I'm always on the lookout for ways to make it more efficient. Our twenty-year-old washer and dryer are the largest drains on the batteries. So when I browsed through *Consumer Reports* recently and saw a write-up about washers and dryers, my interest was immediately captivated.

I read that the new front-loading washing machines use 70 percent less power than the older top-loading machines. Wow! That was a compelling bit of information for an energy-saving enthusiast like me.

"Hey, Sally, take a look at this." I pushed the article over. Sally set down her iron and put on her glasses to take a look. "We could reduce the drain on our batteries with a new washer. Plus it uses only seven to fourteen gallons of hot water instead of the thirty to forty gallons that a top loader uses. Plus it spin dries the clothes at double the rpm of our washer, so the clothes dry a lot faster which saves on energy. This would be great—especially in the winter!"

I was excited with this win-win situation! Sally would get a brand-new washer and dryer, and we could save on our power usage. I had no doubt that Sally would be delighted! I waited eagerly for her face to light up. But it didn't.

Instead, she replied skeptically, "I've done laundry at Matthew and Angela's and at Andrew and Sarah's, and I'm not impressed at all with the new front-loading washers. They use hardly any water, so the clothes can't possibly be as clean. Being clean is really important to me. If you could regulate the water level, it might be a workable option. But as far as I can tell, you can't. Besides, their clothes come out with a lot more wrinkles than mine, which means a lot more ironing time. To be perfectly honest, Jim, I won't have that kind of washer in my home!"

I looked at her incredulously. "Really, honey? That's a pretty strong statement."

"I mean it, Jim. I don't like those washers. I'd rather keep using my old one." Her voice carried that dug-in, "don't push me" tone. She pushed the article back toward me and went on with her ironing. Case closed.

What was wrong with my amiable Sally? She really popped my bubble. Sally doesn't dig in very often, but when she does, it is very hard to budge her. I knew better than to push—at least not right then. I was disappointed. My aspirations for a more efficient system were deflated. But the idea didn't go away. I bided my time.

Soon afterward, we were visiting Matthew and Angela, and I saw Angela bring a load of freshly laundered clothes to the living room to fold while we chatted. It was the perfect opportunity! "Angela, how do you like your front-loading washing machine?"

"Oh, I love it! I grew up with a top loader, and now that I have a front loader, I would hate to go back to the old style. The front loader is so much more gentle on the clothes. They don't wear out so quickly. Also, the front-loading machines are so much more energy efficient, and they use less detergent. So they save money all the way around."

"Do you think they get the clothes as clean as the old top-loading machines? I mean, they use a lot less water, don't they?" I was eyeing Sally out of the corner of my eye and was gratified to see she was listening.

"Oh, I think they get the clothes even cleaner!" Angela was saying just what I wanted her to say. This was perfect.

Then Matthew chimed in. "Father, even though they don't use as much water, they clean better because the action of the front loader is different. The water is forced through the fabric of the clothes, whereas in a top loader, the water just swishes around the surface of the clothes. It's all in the science. You ought to get one! How old is your washer and dryer, anyway? You've had those dinosaurs forever, haven't you? Mother deserves a new one!" I smiled inwardly, but Sally didn't say a word.

At Andrew and Sarah's house, I was able to arrange a similar conversation, but Sally was not convinced. In fact, as we talked on the way home, she reasoned, "How can the clothes be cleaner if you use seventy-five percent less water? If you have dirty clothes, more water gets more dirt out; less water gets less dirt out. My washer agitates vigorously, while their washer tumbles the clothes gently. I don't believe their clothes are cleaner. My whites are whiter than their whites. My eyes tell me what the truth is. I'm not convinced by what they say. I want to use more water than those machines allow you to use—especially since our water comes from a spring and is free and plentiful!"

Now I was not only disappointed, I was irritated. A tinge of self-pity added to my irritation, and a string of thoughts began to rehearse themselves in my head. *Here is all this logical information from five different people she loves, and she still doesn't see it. Maybe it's that she* won't *see it. I'll bet she's just digging in. Her logic makes no sense! Maybe she's an old dog who doesn't want to learn a new trick. After all, she is sixty years old now. What's her problem anyway? She's just like her mother—digs in against all reason. Why can't she think this thing out logically? Seems to me like she's just being stubborn—that's the only reason she can't see it. Her reasoning is just not on target.*

My hands tightened on the steering wheel, and unconsciously, my jaw clenched. I could feel my stomach churning and my blood pressure rising. I dared not say what I was thinking, so I said nothing. But I kept telling myself how bad this situation was and how stupid my wife was acting. *She's the problem! If she only saw things logically, I wouldn't be feeling this way.*

Ever been there? All of us experience times when negative thoughts, feelings, and emotions shape our perception of reality. Anger, depression, resentment, hatred, jealousy, or anxiety all seem like such normal responses when life doesn't deliver what we expect, or, to make it more personal, when the person you're dealing with doesn't respond the way you want them to!

Those negative thoughts and emotions don't ask for our permission to enter, they just barge their way in and demand our obedience. They tell us to lash out or chafe at whatever we see as the cause of the problem. They convince us that if we could change our spouse, our friend, ourselves, our job, or the weather, the problem would be solved. And they tell us that these negative feelings are indispensable in getting this change to take place, that we can't stop feeling the way we're feeling until the situation has changed.

Don't get me wrong. God wired us with the ability to experience a whole kaleidoscope of emotions—both positive and negative—for good, healthy reasons. Experiencing emotions is not the problem. The problem arises when we allow our emotions to rule our reason, to run our lives, to dictate our decisions, and determine our destinies. When emotions rule us, they become part of that pack of preeminence. Rarely, if ever, do they deliver what they promise.

Now you may not wrestle with decisions over a new washer and dryer. But you do agonize over a thousand other topics:

- Getting married
- Buying a new home
- Having children
- Getting a pet
- Choosing an occupation
- Hairstyle

- Music
- Entertainment
- The Internet
- Social gossip
- Sports
- Church issues

And the list goes on and on.

Now ask yourself, Are we Christians really people of the truth? Are we really finishing God's work? Sure, we return our tithes and give offerings. We're involved in evangelism and mission work. We belong to the right church and have cleaned up our lifestyles. But what rules us? Who really is in charge? That's the real question. Am I in charge? Am I the "one"? Or is Christ the "One"?

This is *the issue* that all of us must face if we ever want a way out of the empty mazes of religion, the world, or the self-life. *Who is in charge?*

Most of us avoid this question, but some of us finally get to the point where we recognize the emptiness we are engaged in and our helplessness to get out of it. We are then ready for the answer—and the answer is not in ourselves. It's found in the naked gospel.

Questions to ponder or discuss with others:

1. What is in your pack of preeminence? The approval of others? Self-interest and self-importance?
2. What are the true motivations for what you do? Do you act for the honor and glory of God or for yourself?
3. Do emotions rule your reason, run your life, and dictate your destiny? Does principle go out the window when emotions barge through the door?
4. What really rules you: what's in it for you or what's best for the other person?
5. Who really is in charge? Is it you? Are you the "one"? Or is Christ the "One"?

Chapter 3

The Naked Gospel

In Him we live and move and have our being.

—Acts 17:28

One of the hardest tasks in my life has been to peel away the layers of empty religion to uncover the life-changing gospel. It has been a journey of ups and downs, bumps and potholes, but the conviction has crystallized in my heart that all true believers *in Christ,* both in heaven and on earth, have but one faith.[1] That faith has characterized all of God's true people down through the ages: Abraham, David, Job, Moses, Peter, Paul, Martin Luther, the Waldenses, and a whole host of others who have discovered the essence of true religion. Out of this deep conviction, I have formed my personal statement of faith:

Christianity is Christ.[2] In Christ, regardless of denomination,[3]

---

1. See Ephesians 4:4–6.
2. See 1 Corinthians 2:2; Philippians 1:21.
3. See Ephesians 4:4–6.

there are only blood-bought,[4] born-again,[5] Spirit-led,[6] Bible-believing Christians.[7] Therefore, my creed is the Bible;[8] my empowerment is grace;[9] my life is of faith;[10] my first denomination is Christ;[11] my salvation is in Christ alone.[12]

This is the naked gospel—bare bones, unadorned, irreducible. Christ, and Christ alone, is my salvation every moment of every hour of every day. It is from Him that I receive life. It is in Him that I live and move and have my being. I want to be part of the first denomination, which is defined by a life of faith in Christ. Anything that keeps me from this experience I now view as a bunch of fences, cross fences, barricades, and obstacles. That includes not only the distractions of this world, but also a lot of the Christless theology, religious routines, doctrines, reforms, standards, and professions that can be a substitute for the Savior. In my opinion, whatever fails to bring me into a practical daily experience in Christ, amounts to no saving good.

God made us to be connected to Him, but that connection was lost when Adam and Eve ate the forbidden fruit. Christ came to restore that connection—to reunite us with Him. He was born like you and me, but He never lived outside of His Father's will. He invites us, "Come, walk with Me. I will give you true life!"

The Maytag gospel

After our conversation about the washer and dryer, Sally and I continued down the road in silence. I didn't dare speak, because I knew my thoughts and emotions were leading in the wrong direction. I couldn't believe that any wife in her right mind would refuse the offer of a new washer and dryer—especially with all the evidence I had brought to her about what an improvement they would be over those old antiques. *This is stupid,* I thought. *She's using dinosaur logic.* I was strongly inclined to become more aggressive in my approach. *I'll push her until she gives in. She'll just have to come around to my thinking. That's all there is to it.*

---

4. See Hebrews 9:12–15.
5. See John 3:3–8.
6. See Romans 8:1.
7. See Isaiah 8:20.
8. See Isaiah 8:20.
9. See Ephesians 2:8; 1 Corinthians 15:10, 2 Peter 3:18.
10. See Romans 1:17.
11. See Ephesians 5:23; Matthew 16:18.
12. See Acts 4:12.

Now this was a practical trial of my faith. It's easy to write my statement of faith on the flyleaf of my Bible while I'm sitting alone at my desk in the early morning hours. It's another thing altogether to follow through on that statement of faith when my logic and emotions are relentlessly campaigning for rulership. This is where I come face-to-face with the naked gospel. I have had to make a decision: Who or what was going to be in charge of Jim Hohnberger?

Now think about it with me. What is going to happen if I follow my clamoring emotions? I know from experience, and I suspect you do too. I will become very autocratic with Sally. I'll tell her, not ask her, what we are going to do. Do you know any wife who likes to be treated that way? I don't either. Apart from the naked gospel, Sally would probably respond in one of two ways. She might argue and debate or she might withdraw into cool silence. Either way, the peace and harmony of our home would be shattered.

At that point, my doctrinal positions, church attendance, and vegetarian diet amounted to no saving good, because as James says, "If you have bitter envy and self-seeking in your hearts. . . . This wisdom does not descend from above, but is earthly, sensual, demonic."[13] All my theoretical knowledge of the truth is insufficient to save me from the disaster of my man-managed ways. I need a Savior—Someone outside of myself who can show me a way out!

In all of the mazes I have wandered through, no one ever taught me how personal Christ is. He was always an abstract idea—Someone who lived far away in heaven where He ruled the universe in an austere and autocratic sort of way. Yet, the essence of the naked gospel is that "the high and lofty One that inhabiteth eternity, whose name is Holy" dwells not only "in the high and holy place, [but] with him also that is of a contrite and humble spirit, to revive the spirit of the humble, and to revive the heart of the contrite ones."[14] Jesus means it when He says, "I will never leave you nor forsake you."[15] And He's not joking when He promises, "I will instruct you and teach you in the way you should go; I will guide you with My eye."[16]

When do I most need Jesus? All the time—especially when I'm alone with my wife talking about washers and dryers. Are you with me?

I used to react to my emotions automatically; there wasn't even a nanosecond between my emotion rising and my acting on it. But God has been working with me over the years to teach me that I have a choice. I don't have to surrender to those destructive habits. The most effective prayer I have learned to use in these

---

13. James 3:14, 15.
14. Isaiah 57:15, KJV.
15. Hebrews 13:5.
16. Psalm 32:8.

situations is simply: "Lord, what would *Thou* have me to do?"[17]

"Jim, 'Abide in Me, and I in you. As the branch cannot bear fruit of itself, unless it abides in the vine, neither can you, unless you abide in Me.' Jim, let Me prune some of your thoughts and emotions, so that the fruit of the Spirit can appear."[18]

Galatians 5:22, 23 lists nine fruits that will be seen in our lives when God is preeminent. The first three—love, joy, and peace—concern our attitude toward God. When we enter into peace with Him, His love and joy are ours. The second three fruits—patience, kindness, and goodness—deal with our social relationships. How do we treat those who try our patience the most? What is our attitude and approach toward them? We must remember what Jesus said—that He would not break a bruised reed or snuff out a smoking flax.[19] The third set of fruits—faithfulness, gentleness, and self-control—describe principles that guide our conduct. Regardless of others' actions or perceptions, we must operate within the boundaries of faithfulness, gentleness, and self-control.

The principles of God's Word outline His path for me to follow, and His Spirit works with me to show me, in practical terms, how to walk in that path. God promises, "Your ears shall hear a word behind you, saying, 'This is the way, walk in it.' "[20] Now I have never heard God speak to me audibly, but He speaks to me all the time through my conscience. And He does to you as well.

"Jim, loosen your grip on the steering wheel. That's it. Now take some deep breaths and let the tension go. That's better. Now think about the pleasant time you just had with your family. Good. Now, why don't you look over at Sally and smile. In fact, reach over and take her hand. Let this issue go."

Pruning is not fun. It's painful to have my man-managed thoughts cut away. There is something in every one of us that resists this process, and God never forces it on us. But we must submit to it if we want to enjoy the benefits of His life flowing through us to produce the luscious fruits of the Spirit.

I cooperated and let the issue go. I said *No* to running my own show and *Yes* to God—and that meant letting go of my desire for energy efficiency (which is a big deal for me) and my "rightness" (which is an even bigger deal).

Lord, I queried, *will we have to live with antique laundry equipment until our dying day?*

"Just trust Me, Jim. Trust Me and stay in the path I have laid out for you."

---

17. See Acts 9:6.
18. John 15:4; see also John 15:1–5.
19. See Matthew 12:20.
20. Isaiah 30:21.

Round two

The next morning, God spoke to my conscience (that's an actual ongoing part of His grace).

"Jim, go to the Web site for Consumer Reports *and look up washers and dryers."*

I did.

As I studied the Web page on washers and dryers, I asked, "Lord, I already know all this information. What do You want me to do with it?"

Then I noticed a link to a video showing the difference between the efficiency of top-loading and front-loading machines. The video scientifically proved that front loaders cleaned better, were gentler on the clothes, and used less power and water to do it than top loaders. Wonderful!

"Lord, do I have Your permission to share this with Sally?"

"Yes, Jim. Just be sure to stay on the path of faithfulness, gentleness, and self-control."

I was excited. All my hopes for energy efficiency sprang to new life. This video was so objective, so scientific, and so convincing that I was sure Sally would see the light.

"Thank You, Lord! You are so good. You have really shown me the way through this one!"

The only problem was that Sally was not impressed. How could that be? The evidence in favor of front loaders was incontrovertible! *I'm right! I know I'm right! How can she be so stubborn?* As Sally stood behind me at my computer, all my old emotions came back like a flood, and the temptation was stronger than ever to simply push my way onto her.

You know what I'm talking about, don't you? Can't you just feel my rising blood pressure? You've been there too. Maybe not with washing machines, but other issues push your hot buttons. What do your emotions drive your reason to conclude? Do you feel like compelling the other person to accept your view of things? Maybe you have the opposite weakness. Are you driven by timidity and a poor self-image? Do you give in to another person's wishes simply to avoid conflict?

The naked gospel always allows for individuality—both our own and the other person's. It never forces or compels. The born-again experience always consults with God, His principles, and His approach. The bottom-line issue here is not who is right, but who is willing to look beyond his or her own interests for the sake of the other. Who is willing to say, "Lord, what would *Thou* have me to do?"[21]

Problems inevitably occur in all relationships. Have you noticed that? We'd

---

21. See Acts 9:6.

like to get rid of the problems (that is, the other person's way of thinking or acting, which is different than ours) so we can be in harmony. But that's not the real
basis of peace. The Bible says, "If we walk in the light, God himself being the
light, we also experience a shared life with one another."[22] When problems arise
in a relationship, is your focus on bringing the other party around to your perspective? Or is your focus on walking in the light with God?

So there I am at my computer, and my blood pressure is rising by the second.
Yes, I accept the Scriptures as the sole rule of my life, but will I now let these holy
principles have sway and walk with God in the light? Or am I going to be in
charge? Will I stay on the path of faithfulness, gentleness, and self-control or will
I assert my rightness and bring my unreasonable wife into line?

*Lord, why did You lead me to share this video with Sally if You knew it was only
going to put me back in this awful dilemma?*

*"It's good practice for you, Jim! Just trust Me and stay on the path I've laid out for
you."*

What should I do, then, Lord?

"Just look up at her, smile, and thank her for taking a look at the video."

*That's all, Lord? Can't I jab at her just a little bit for being just like her mother?
Can't I reflect back to her how antiquated her logic is?*

"That's not safe ground for you right now, Jim. Trust Me. Lay it all down."

I had to lay down my "rights" and hopes again! I had to let go of the irritation
I felt at Sally for not seeing the situation correctly. I had to set aside my lawyer
logic and my negative thoughts about her intelligence. In short, I had to be willing to allow God to walk me through this. All the self-oriented thoughts, feelings,
and emotions had to die. And now I had to trust God to give me peace regardless
of the outcome. This is what it means to walk with God daily!

A creative alternative

About a week later, I was flipping through the mail as I walked back from
the mailbox. A sale catalogue from Vann's Appliance Store caught my eye. I
was amazed! We never get anything from Vann's. Guess which washers and
dryers were on sale?

All my energy-loving dreams reignited. I picked up my pace and burst
through the back door into the kitchen where Sally was preparing lunch. "Sally!
Look what we got in the mail!"

I held the advertisement in front of her while she diced cucumbers. Without missing a stroke with her deft little knife, she glanced at the ad and said,
"Hmm."

---

22. 1 John 1:7, *The Message.*

Is that all you can say? I thought to myself. Out loud I said, "Sally, this is the washer and dryer we've been talking about. It's on sale, and we never get ads from Vann's. This could be God smiling on us!"

Sally gave me a sideways look and commented dryly, "Jim, even if it's on sale, my mind hasn't changed. I'd rather keep what I already like."

"Sally, what wife wouldn't be excited that her husband wants to buy her a brand-new washer and dryer? Why can't you be normal?"

Sally didn't respond, and God called for my heart: *"Jim, do you want to continue down that path? You know where it will lead."*

Leaving the scene of action, I retreated to my office to pray and regroup.

Then a creative idea suddenly occurred to me. I toyed with it for a moment and then discarded it. *That's stupid. No merchant in his right mind would go for that!* I started working through the rest of the mail. But the idea kept coming back to my mind. "Lord, is that You?" Finally, as an act of faith, I called the appliance store.

"Hi! I just received your ad in the mail, and I'm considering the front-loading washer and dryer you have advertised on sale."

"Yes, how can I help you?" The salesman was pleasant and professional sounding.

"Well, my wife is not convinced that she would like the front-loading washer as well as she likes her top loader. So I wanted to ask if you would consider letting her try the machines with the option to return them if she doesn't like them."

There! I had gotten the idea out. I kind of winced while I waited for the response, but I was surprised.

"Sure! We can offer you a fifteen-day customer satisfaction guarantee. If your wife doesn't like them, just call us, and we'll come pick up the machines."

"Would you charge us a re-stocking fee if we take you up on the return?"

"No, sir. There's no risk or cost to you if your wife is not completely satisfied."

I asked a few more questions and clarified some details. It was all settled! I was excited—again! I ran down the stairs to look for Sally. By this time, she was out weeding the flower bed along the driveway. As I approached, she smiled up at me and said, "I know what you're going to say—and, yes, I'd be willing to give it a try."

"How did you know?" I asked.

Glancing to my open study window just above us, she chuckled, "I heard the whole conversation."

Success at last! Sally won! Jim won! God won! Our marriage won—and we lived happily ever after!

Not really. Life always presents new hurdles to cross. But God promises, "I will never leave you nor forsake you." So we may boldly say, "The LORD is my helper; I will not fear [when my wife doesn't see things my way]."[23] The only thing we need to fear is taking our hand out of His.

God worked with me just like He worked with Daniel. Of course, the situation Daniel faced in the court of Nebuchadnezzar was much more important than mine. Life and limb were on the line for him, whereas only a few watts were on the line for me. But Daniel faced a delicate dilemma: eat the food offered to an idol and blaspheme the God he loved, or refuse to eat it and be executed. Two options—neither acceptable to an aspiring, young, dedicated nobleman. Even though he couldn't see the way out, when Daniel asked God for help, God gave him a creative alternative—and it worked! Daniel won. Nebuchadnezzar won. And God won.

How many problems do we face that seem to have only lose-lose options? We can't see any other way. But God can. He can see doors where we see only dead ends. That's the naked gospel—God at work in my life through His Word, His grace, and His truth. As we cooperate with His work in our lives, "we live and move and have our being" in Him![24]

Now when you possess the naked gospel and it is generally working in your life, go ahead and put some clothes on it. Do our naked bodies need clothes? Of course! Please don't go without them! But the clothes are not us. In the same way, the gospel is dressed in doctrines, lifestyle reforms, proper biblical church affiliation, evangelism, and missions. (But the attire of the gospel should never replace the gospel itself.) When this is true, the outward attire is no longer a barrier to divide and separate us. Rather, it challenges us to a better understanding of His thoughts and ways.

Christianity is Christ

Once a month, our ministry sends out an e-mail to encourage our readers. One of the most popular ones contained the image shown on the next page.

A picture is worth a thousand words, isn't it? There's nothing particularly wrong with all those dark lightbulbs, is there? They just need to be connected to the power source. No lightbulb can be a substitute for electricity. But when the invisible power of the electric current flows through the filament, a glow of radiant light floods the darkness.

That's the naked gospel. When the power of God flows into me, it lights up

---

23. Hebrews 13:5, 6.
24. Acts 17:28.

Christianity is Christ!

or your doctrines.

your lifestyle...

your outreach...

your knowledge...

It is not your church...

It is Christ in you,
your only hope of glory.

my life. The naked gospel is about belonging to God[25] and being breathed into by God.[26] It's all about God's life flowing into me and creating "goodness, righteousness, and truth" where there was none before.[27] It's learning to appropriate in my life what has been provided for me through the life, death, and resurrection of Christ.[28]

The naked gospel frees me from the maze of self. It lifts that old pack of preeminence off my shoulders and liberates me from the issue of self. It guides me through that dusty, narrow old door where few venture.

The narrow way

Jesus forewarned us about the mazes of life, and He wants to show us the way out. Listen to His words: "Enter by the narrow gate; for wide is the gate and broad is the way that leads to destruction, and there are many who go in by it. Because narrow is the gate and difficult is the way which leads to life, and there are few who find it."[29]

---

25. See Galatians 2:20.
26. See Genesis 2:7.
27. See Ephesians 2:10; Ephesians 5:9.
28. See Romans 6.
29. Matthew 7:13, 14.

Don't be deceived. It is possible to be in the broad way when you think you are in the narrow way. I call it the "gospel of substitution." Many—if not the majority of people—mistakenly believe that they are in the narrow way when, in reality, they have missed the essence of the gospel. This gospel of substitution contains a lot of good, a lot of energy, and a lot of focus. But it is missing the core, and it leaves you wandering the endless mazes of religion, while still wearing that pack of preeminence.

The gospel of substitution can be

- your church and your pew
- your doctrine
- your outreach, evangelism, and missions
- your lifestyle
- your reforms
- your church attendance
- your knowledge, facts, and truths
- your good works

The gospel of substitution can even be your nonconformity to all these things. If your gospel does not remove your preeminence and bring you into a life of surrender to Christ and practical dependence in Him, beware!

Let's go back to Betty, Chris, the rich young ruler, Allen, Bill, Joan, and of course, me. All of us were connected to a visible church, which is right and good. We all possessed a lifestyle above that of the world—praise God! We all subscribed to a distinctive platform of truth and believed in taking the gospel to the world, which is the gospel commission. Yet something was seriously amiss! The heartbeat of the saving gospel was weak, thready, and, in some cases, even absent.

That's nothing new. In Christ's day, the religious leaders were so enamored with their dead externals that when the very Heart of true religion was offered to them and stood before them, they crucified Him. They were "in charge" of their religion. Just read the sad history in the four Gospels of how church-attending, truth-wielding, lifestyle-exacting, prophecy-knowing believers all missed it.

Are we missing it today? Yes, I believe we are! I believe we need to seriously examine ourselves in the light of the naked gospel. Do we possess it or do we merely profess it? Have we come to terms with the packs of preeminence we all carry around with us? Have we laid them at the Savior's feet and stepped through that dusty, narrow old door? Is the heart of Christ beating in us? Is His truth our foundation? Does His Spirit have management of us?

Do we know ourselves?

Appliance exam

The Bible admonishes me to examine myself—not my wife or anyone else. Why? Because I can do something about only one person—me! It says, "Examine yourselves as to whether you are in the faith. Test yourselves."[30]

Am I in the faith? How do I know? Jesus gave us an unerring test: we can know by our fruit.[31] Do we bear the fruit of the Spirit or carry out the works of our flesh? I don't always like that test. It cuts so close to my heart. I'd prefer testing myself by the "gospel of right" (which is one of the main branches of the gospel of substitution)! Are you with me? There's a big difference, you know, between the two. One has Christ as its head. The other rules through knowledge.

The gospel of right is very dangerous—because it is so right. It seems so right to be right, especially when we've got the right facts, the right information, the right truths, the right reforms, and the right outreach. When we live by the power of right, it is so easy to deceive ourselves that *we're* all right. Why? Because, of course, *we're right!*

When I landed on the idea of replacing our washer and dryer, I had all the facts on my side. I had science to back me up. I had my sons and their wives to back me up. I had *Consumer Reports* to back me up. According to the gospel of right, I was right! However, according to the faith of Jesus Christ, I was wrong. My rightness became my pack of preeminence, and I had to take it off more than once to step through that dusty, narrow old door. When we hold the truth in unrighteousness, we are not in the faith of Jesus![32] In fact, it has been said that the saints do their greatest sinning when they believe they are right!

We must live by the power of God![33] Christ must be in charge—not us! He is our head—not truth. The Holy Spirit must be our life.[34] This is the electric current that comes from outside of us and lights up our lives. Then truth is our foundation rather than our god.

When I examined myself, when I tested my fruit, it wasn't Christ in me; it was "right facts" in me. I was preeminent in my facts. I had to listen to God whispering to my conscience by and through His Holy Spirit according to His Word. I had to submit all my thoughts, feelings, and emotions to be laundered by Him. I had to allow grace to empower me. Then, by faith, I surrendered my will to His and placed my dependence upon Him to help me

---

30. 2 Corinthians 13:5.
31. Matthew 7:20.
32. Romans 1:18.
33. See 2 Corinthians 13:4.
34. See Romans 8:1.

change my approach. When I cooperated with Him, God had a way of settling the disparity between Sally and myself that I never would have thought of on my own—a fifteen-day customer satisfaction guarantee. Thank You, Lord!

That's not the end of the story, though, I have to confess. Vann's Appliance Store delivered our brand-new front-loading washer and matching dryer. They looked really cool in our laundry room!

As soon as the machines were hooked up, Sally started experimenting. I just knew she was going to love them! Well, to make a long story short, she didn't. In all fairness, she spent hours with the machines. She would get down on the floor and peer into the window with a flashlight to see how much water was sloshing around and how the clothes were being agitated. This confirmed her worst fears. There was very little water in there—not even a puddle—and the drum turned back and forth very slowly. "How can that get the clothes as clean as my top loader?" she questioned again. On top of that, the wash cycle took an hour and a half to two hours to run instead of the forty-five minutes the old machine took—and my generator had to be running that entire time. These machines might save energy with a conventional power system, but they didn't with my off-the-grid power system.

The big test came the day she washed our white sheets. I use a prescription skin cream that stains the sheets yellow. Sally agitates them for forty-five minutes in bleach in her top loader every other week to get them pure white. The new washer allowed her to add bleach only to the first rinse cycle. The sheets came out only 80 percent clean. She tried adding the bleach to the wash cycle. They were only slightly cleaner.

Sally really gave it an honest try. She even went down to the appliance store and chatted with the salesman and repairman to see if she could get around some of the water-saving features. The old appliance repairman confirmed Sally's perspective. He told her, "You will never find a new washer on the market that cleans clothes as well as the old top loaders. The new ones are built according to new government regulations, and they are designed to use less water and less energy with recyclable material. They simply don't clean as well and have to be replaced more often."

Long before the fifteen-day trial expired, Sally and I both concluded that she was right. We called up Vann's and ordered a new top loader to exchange for the front loader. On my power system, it saves more energy than either the front loader or the old top loader, so I'm happy. Sally's happy because she can use all the hot water she wants to get the laundry spiffy clean. And God's happy because He won over our flesh.

I relearned a lesson I've had to face more than once: just because I *think* I'm right doesn't mean I *am* right. Our dependence must be in God—not in our rightness.

Jesus issued a solemn warning for the adherents of the gospel of right in Matthew 7:21–23:

> Not every one that saith unto me, Lord, Lord, shall enter into the kingdom of heaven; but he that doeth the will of my Father which is in heaven. Many will say to me in that day, Lord, Lord, have we not prophesied in thy name? and in thy name have cast out devils? and in thy name done many wonderful works? And then will I profess unto them, I never knew you: depart from me, ye that work iniquity (KJV).

Is it possible to be involved in a spectacular ministry, to be a member of God's church, to use the authority of the Scriptures and the name of Jesus Christ, and yet be missing the naked gospel? Yes, it is. The danger of self-deception is high. We can put service in place of the Savior, slip into our pews instead of hanging our dependence on Him, and get into our pulpits—whatever our pet topic or issue is—rather than face that pack of preeminence. All of us—you, me, Betty, Chris, Allen, Bill, and Joan—need to test ourselves often to know whether we are in the faith—or if we have substituted something in place of Christ.

Do you see the naked gospel? Do you want it? Then God is calling. Do you have an ear to hear?

Questions to ponder or discuss with others:

1. How many layers of empty religion are keeping you from the life-changing gospel?
2. Do you possess the naked gospel in your daily living?
3. When God whispers the way to your conscience, do you follow?
4. Do you allow for others' individuality?
5. Do you look to God for creative alternatives?
6. Do you take your hand out of God's hand? How many times a day?
7. Are you "in charge" of your religion?
8. Do you possess the naked gospel or merely profess it?
9. Have you come to terms with the pack of preeminence you carry?
10. Are you afraid to truly examine yourself?
11. Is it possible to be involved in a spectacular ministry, to be a member of God's church, to use the authority of the Scriptures and the name of Jesus Christ, and yet be missing the naked gospel?

Chapter 4

God Calling

"He who has ears to hear, let him hear!"

—Matthew 13:9

*J*esus deserves our unending admiration, focus, and affection. When He wiped out our debt by absorbing our punishment, He proved Himself to be a friend without equal. Today, He intercedes for us and acts as our personal Advocate, providing for us what no mere religion or system of belief could ever offer. He has given Himself to be the solution to our every problem. Therefore, we are admonished more than a dozen times in the New Testament: "He who has ears to hear, let him hear."[1]

God is not saying that we should expect to hear Him audibly, although there are times when we might wish God would break the silence and speak audibly to us. Rather, for those who really want to hear, God can be heard speaking constantly.[2] Our problem is not that God is not speaking, but rather, that we're not listening. Let me illustrate.

---

1. Matthew 11:15; see also Matthew 13:9, 43; Mark 4:9, 23; 7:16; Luke 8:8; 14:35; Revelation 2:7, 11, 17, 29; 3:6, 13, 22; 13:9.

2. Psalm 19.

Fingers in our ears

Dennis was frustrated big time. He and I took a walk between meetings at one of our annual Empowered Living camp meetings. It was a crisp autumn day, and the fallen leaves on the forest trail crunched pleasantly under our feet. Dennis didn't take long to get to the point. "Jim, I bought your CD seminar *Why Country Living?* several years ago, and our family was convinced that we needed to move to a quieter country setting, so that we could listen to God better."

"Praise God!" I interjected.

"But, Jim, our house has been on the market for over two years now, and we have not received even one offer. Not one! Why doesn't God answer my prayers? Why doesn't God hear me? You say God speaks to you and that He's no respecter of persons."

I nodded in agreement.

"Well, why doesn't He speak to me? I'm listening, but there's total silence. It's like He ignores me. I don't get it. Doesn't He want us to move to a quieter environment?"

Dennis was frustrated—as are a lot of people I talk to. While I don't have all the answers, I know God does. So at that moment, I petitioned God silently, *Help me, Lord, to help this man. You have the answers. I don't.*

Then this thought came to my mind, and I shared it with Dennis. "Many people today are looking for answers. They have one ear pointed to heaven with their hand cupped around it. They are saying, 'Speak, Lord. Show me what I need to know. I want to hear from You. Please, Lord, speak.' "

Dennis nodded, listening intently. "Yes," he agreed. "That's me."

I continued. "But that's only part of the picture. In their other ear, people have a finger. Now the surest way to get an answer to the ear that is cupped toward heaven is to pull your finger out of your other ear and *listen* to what God is calling to you in that ear."

Dennis suddenly turned pale, and then an astonished expression spread over his face. He was speechless, so I gently asked him, "Is there something God has been convicting you about that you are refusing to cooperate with?"

He hesitated only momentarily and then replied, "Yes!"

I asked him, "Do you want to share it with me?"

"Pornography. I'm addicted to pornography."

God had been calling to Dennis's heart, but the call about pornography was not the call Dennis wanted to hear. He was afraid of it. He didn't comprehend the freedom God had in store for him. You see, God knows His sheep and answers our prayers according to our real needs! Dennis's real need was dealing with his addiction to pornography—not his perceived need of a new location.

God was calling to him as He does to all His sheep. However, we must follow. We must actively cooperate. "My sheep hear My voice, and I know them, and they follow Me."[3]

"Dennis, the best way to have your prayer answered is to deal with the known call of God upon your heart in the present. Would you like some guidance on how to face your addiction?"

He did, and I shared with him God's principles for finding freedom.[4] I ran into Dennis about a year later at the same camp meeting, and he updated me. "Jim, I'm free of pornography! Praise God! And . . . my house has sold! We're moving to our country property in just a few weeks! Praise God, and thank you for helping me to see myself as I really was."

"I'm delighted to hear that, Dennis! Facing your addiction didn't earn God's favor. It simply untied His hands, so that He could pour out more blessings on you."

Many of us have tied God's hands from answering our own prayers. How? By refusing to listen to Him in the known areas of His revealed will as expressed in His Word. Hebrews 12:25 says, "See that you do not refuse Him who speaks."

God had been speaking to Dennis, but Dennis wasn't listening or following. He was refusing God in known areas. How then could God speak to him in unknown areas and bless him in new endeavors? If God had moved Dennis to the country while he was living in known sin, with that bundle of preeminence being in charge, God would have been his enabler rather than his Savior.

Are you refusing God? Are you the one in charge? Are you the preeminent one in your life, or is God? If you are, you will most likely have a hard time hearing Him at any of what I classify as the three different levels of God's call to us as individuals.

Three levels

As the triangle to the right illustrates, level one is the essential foundation for the next two levels. The second level builds on the first and prepares us for level three. (Mind you, this is for discussion purposes only. No one can diagram exactly how or when God will, or will not, speak to them. God is God and does what He wishes when

---

3. John 10:27.

4. For more information about overcoming sexual addiction, please see my book *Men of Power,* particularly chapter 12, "Touching the Taboo."

He wishes. However, these levels will help us understand how we can unplug our ears, so that we are not blocking His voice to our hearts.)

From our side of the equation, level one is the place to begin. If you, like Dennis, are having trouble hearing God at level three, make sure your ear is open to level one. Dennis was attempting to hear God calling to him at the third level while he wasn't cooperating with God at the first level. God clearly says, "If I regard iniquity in my heart, the Lord will not hear."[5]

Level one—educating my conscience

God speaks to us constantly through the Scriptures. If you want to know God and become acquainted with His voice, study His Word. Jesus said of the Old Testament Scriptures (and how much more is it true of the New): "These are they which testify of Me,"[6] the Redeemer, the One who is able to  save us from our packs of preeminence and deliver us from all our empty mazes. Yes, the whole Bible tells of Christ. From the first record of Creation—"without Him nothing was made that was made"—to the closing promise—"behold, I am coming quickly"[7]—we are reading of His works and listening to His voice.

It is vitally important to recognize that God speaks to us *personally* through His Word. In all of His promises and warnings, He means me. God so loved the world, that He gave His only-begotten Son, that *I* by believing in Him, might not perish, but have everlasting life.[8] The experiences related in God's Word are to be *my* experiences. The prayers recorded are meant to be my own. The precepts taught are meant for me personally. "*I* have been crucified with Christ; it is no longer I who live, but Christ lives in *me;* and the life which I now live in the flesh I live by the faith in the Son of God, who loved *me* and gave Himself for *me*."[9]

God was speaking clearly to Dennis in Proverbs 5:20, 5, 8: "Why wilt thou, my son, be ravished with a strange woman?" "Her feet go down to death; her steps take hold on hell. . . . Remove thy way far from her" (KJV).

If you have access to the Scriptures, you can never say that God does not speak to you. Open His Word. Unplug your ears. Let Him speak to your heart and the issues of your life. Surrender to His ways and will.

5. Psalm 66:18.

6. John 5:39.

7. John 1:3; Revelation 22:12.

8. See John 3:16.

9. Galatians 2:20; emphasis added.

I set aside the first part of every morning to read my Bible for two primary reasons. First, to understand and surrender to God's revealed will for my life and character. Second, to educate my conscience, so that when God speaks to me during the day, I will recognize His call to my heart as distinct from my own human reasoning or the enemy's suggestions.

"To the law and to the testimony! If they do not speak according to this word, it is because there is no light in them."[10] Not every thought that comes to me is worthy of considering. All our thoughts, impressions, and ideas need to be filtered through God's principles. If they do not violate His Word, we may consider them and go forward with His Holy Spirit guiding us. If they are at odds with Holy Scripture, we should dismiss them and have nothing to do with them.

I recently heard about someone who struggled with the implications of the fourth commandment for her life. She wrestled with it until she decided to put out a fleece. *If God wants me to keep the fourth commandment,* she thought, *He should make His will known to me by giving me a special sign.* When the sign was not forthcoming, she decided that God was granting her a special dispensation to ignore the commandment. I beg to differ with her. When God's will is plainly stated in His Word, instead of praying for God to confirm to us what He has already stated, we ought to pray for grace to conform our lives to His will.

Just as the base of a triangle is the foundation of the shape, so hearing God's voice through His Word is the foundation, the basis, of walking with Him. It is of utmost importance that we all become proficient in level one before we focus on the next two levels. If someone plans to learn algebra and geometry, shouldn't he or she first master addition and subtraction (level one), then multiplication and division (level two) before they can master algebra and geometry (level three)?

God does not always approach us in the order of these levels, however. There are times when He works with us at level two or level three in order to bring us to a surrender in level one. God wants our hearts and pursues us according to His own unsearchable ways. But we are talking about our side of the equation: "You will seek Me and find Me, when you search for Me with *all* your heart!"[11]

Are all your known choices presently surrendered to God's revealed will? Have you searched the Scriptures to understand God's principles related to the areas of your life in which you want answers? If His will is plainly stated there, don't look for another answer.

This process takes time. The treadmill pace of the twenty-first century is

---

10. Isaiah 8:20.
11. Jeremiah 29:13; emphasis added.

designed by the devil to make sure you do not have the time in your schedule or the room in your brain to contemplate God's principles and how they relate to the way you think, respond to life, and relate to those about you.

God calls us to "be still and know" that He is God.[12] He does not change His ways for our fast-paced lifestyle. No, we must adapt our lives to His revealed will and way! We all must turn away from a life of ceaseless activity. "My people will dwell in a *peaceful* habitation, in *secure* dwellings, and in *quiet* resting places."[13] "Aspire to lead a *quiet* life."[14]

No, we don't need to join a monastery or become hermits. But we do need to find a balance in life that prioritizes time for God on a consistent basis. (We will discuss how to do that in greater detail in chapter 7.) Why? Because it is in the silence of the soul that God's voice is made more distinct.

Level two—learning to listen

God is always there for us! Period.[15] He is as available to us as the air we breathe. We all have the privilege of coming to know an omniscient, omnipresent, and omnipotent God. He calls Himself *El Shaddai*—the All-sufficient One![16]

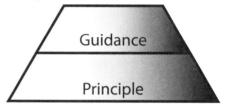

He's all-sufficient for all of us! He's omniscient—that means He has all the answers and sees everything in advance of it happening. He's acquainted with all our ways and comprehends our path in advance. He knows even the word on our tongue beforehand.[17] Infinitely knowing! Infinitely seeing! That's our God! Wow! I want to connect with a God like that.

He's also omnipresent. He's with you even if you're Jonah in the belly of a whale. He's with you in the fiery furnace like He was with Shadrach, Meshach, and Abed-Nego. If they banish you to a desert island as they did John, He's there. "Where can I go from Your Spirit? Or where can I flee from Your presence?"[18] What a God!

He's omnipotent. He possesses infinite power. He speaks worlds into

---

12. Psalm 46:10.

13. Isaiah 32:18; emphasis added.

14. 1 Thessalonians 4:11; emphasis added.

15. See Hebrews 13:5, 6; Matthew 28:20.

16. See Exodus 6:2, 3.

17. See Psalm 139:3, 4.

18. Psalm 139:7.

existence. He parts the Red Sea by a mere thought. He has unlimited power over everything, but He limits His power over our will, because He values the right and the ability He has instilled within each of us to say Yes or No to Him. Praise God!

Inside information

God offers you and me the benefits of His inside information—if we choose to listen to Him. That doesn't mean He discloses to us everything He sees and knows; it means that He leads us as we would choose to be led if we understood our own hearts and saw ourselves as He does. He offers this guidance free of charge to all who choose to connect, listen, and follow. Often He whispers quietly to our consciences, calls unobtrusively to our hearts, or makes a suggestion to our minds. However you want to refer to it, that is God calling. Will you respond? Do you want the inside information He offers? How often we all dismiss God's call to our hearts. I have. You have. We all have. But God lives to serve you and me every day of our lives.

Have you ever been just sitting there, when all of a sudden you sense a call to your heart to do something nice for your spouse? That's God! He speaks to you through His Holy Spirit. He knows how to keep love alive and tries to get your attention.

Have you ever been thinking about someone you haven't seen in a long time and are suddenly impressed to call him or her? I have, and when I called, the person said, "How did you know I was hurting?" That's God who is speaking to your heart!

There's no such thing as a coincidence. He wants to use us as His instruments to serve. Have you ever been in a difficult situation and had no clue what to say or how to fix it, and then the answer came? That's God.

"He cares for you"[19]—all the time, through every situation, in every detail both large and small.

Direction for daily living

It was a warm July afternoon—a perfect day for washing my SUV. I gave the vehicle premium attention both inside and out, rolling down the windows while I finished the interior. When the job was done, I backed the SUV into the garage. As I stepped out of the vehicle, a thought came to my mind: *"Close all the windows."*

I thought to myself, *That's not necessary. The weather is perfect. It would be good*

---

19. 1 Peter 5:7.

to let the fresh air circulate through the vehicle.

I continued on to my next project, but the thought impressed itself on me again: *"Jim, roll up all the windows."* I considered the idea momentarily and then reasoned it away. It just didn't seem important.

A few hours later, I needed Sally. She wasn't in the house, so I went outside and called for her. She answered right away. "Jim, I'm upstairs in the garage."

As I entered the garage, I nearly choked. Dust was everywhere. "Sally, what are you doing?"

"Oh, I'm just cleaning up the attic a bit and decided to sweep it out. It was pretty dirty when I started, but it's looking a lot better now. Come up and see."

I didn't doubt that things were looking better up there, but they sure weren't looking better down below! A thick layer of dust and debris coated my newly washed SUV; and yes, it had sifted easily through the open windows and made a mess of the interior.

My jaw dropped open, and some very choice words were about to make themselves vocal when God called to my heart: *"Jim, Sally is innocent. It won't make your SUV any cleaner to chew her out. Besides, then you'll have two messes to clean up—the one in your vehicle and the one in your marriage. And remember how I encouraged you to roll up your windows?*[20] *I knew this was coming and tried to save you some double work, but you negated My advance call to your present need."*

My mouth clamped shut. "Oh Lord, will I ever learn to fully recognize You in the moment?"

Do you want God's guidance? I do! He promises, "I will instruct you and teach you in the way you should go; I will guide you with My eye."[21] We must begin learning, through experience, how to distinguish God's calling in regard to our everyday needs. Failing to do that can have serious consequences.

Disaster that God wanted to avert

I was invited to a friend's home for a work bee. Fred, Burt, and I arrived first and were busy cutting down brush, trimming the lower dead branches off the trees, and stacking all of it to be burned later in the fall. It was a hot August day, and the sweat was pouring down our faces and soaking our shirts.

Mark arrived later than the rest of us. As he parked his pickup near ours, his young German shepherd, Blitz, caught sight of the activity and got excited. Mark was concerned that his friendly dog might get in the way—or worse yet, meet the unfriendly side of one of our chainsaws or axes. So, against Blitz's protests, Mark left him inside the truck.

---

20. See Isaiah 30:21.
21. Psalm 32:8.

As he shut the pickup door and grabbed his chainsaw from the bed of the truck, he was impressed to open the windows of the truck slightly.

No, he thought. *I can't stay long, anyway. Blitz will be OK.*

As he walked toward us, the thought again pricked his conscience: *"Crack the windows for ventilation."*

Again he reasoned it away. He really felt he'd be there only a little while.

Two hours later, as he headed back toward his truck, he noticed that Blitz was not watching for him as usual. A feeling of dread came over him, and he rushed to the truck and jerked open the door. There was Blitz on the floor— unconscious and barely breathing.

Mark yelled to us, and we all came running. One of us called the vet while Mark tried to rouse his dog. Over the phone, the vet gave some first aid instructions for heat exhaustion, and Mark did all he could while I drove them both to the animal hospital.

The vet did everything he knew to revive poor Blitz, but it was to no avail. Mark and his family lost a beautiful and beloved pet that day, because Mark tuned out God's call to his conscience.

I often marvel at God's care for us. He gets involved even with the small details of our lives and wants to save us from many of our foolish mistakes if only we will habituate ourselves to listen to Him calling and allow Him to be on the throne of our thoughts and feelings and actions.

Level three—a process of discovery

God has ways of directing our futures that we cannot predict. Exodus 14:14 states, "The Lord will fight for you, and you shall hold your peace." God wants to fight for us and is answering our prayers, but so often we inadvertently resist His providence. We don't recognize it for what it really is.

For me, asking God to reveal His will for my future is a process of discovery, a process of waiting upon the Lord to show His divine hand directing my future.[22]

More than twenty-five years ago, Sally and I sold our prosperous business and most of our stuff and moved with our two young boys from suburban Wisconsin to the wil-

derness of Montana. We wanted to find a real walk with God that changed us from the inside out. Following our move, we had eighteen thousand dollars left.

22. See Psalm 130:5.

We budgeted this amount to last for three years, so that I could focus my time and energies on God, my marriage, and my boys.[23]

We eventually reached the point where our meager funds were running out. I needed to provide for my family, but what does one do in a remote mountain valley to generate an income? Levels one and two were in operation to the best that I understood them, and I was actively praying for God to show His divine hand in my need of employment.

One day, while Sally and I were in town shopping in the local grocery store, we bumped into Paul, a realtor who had showed us some country properties three years earlier.

"Hi, Jim and Sally! I've thought about you two from time to time and wondered whatever became of you. Did you find something to buy in this area?"

"We did, Paul. A private owner north of Polebridge offered to sell us his little log cabin, and that's where we are now."

"Well, how's it going?"

We briefly shared the events of the three years since we had last seen him—the walk with God we were finding and how it was revitalizing our marriage and connecting our family together.

Paul listened to me intently. When I finished, he paused a moment and then looked me in the eye. "Jim, I'd like you to sell real estate for me in your remote valley."

My mind sized up the situation very quickly and came to a decision.

"No, Paul. There's nothing up there to sell. Either the United States Forestry Service or Glacier National Park owns ninety-eight percent of the land. I think it would be a waste of my time and yours."

"Don't be so sure about that, Jim. There's more up there than meets the eye. Think about it, will you?"

A few days later, a letter from Paul arrived at my home, asking me to stop by his office. It made no sense to me, but I took the matter to God anyway. I was unusually impressed to at least stop by his office and thank him for his consideration, but my answer was No. I didn't want to get roped into the round of meetings and fees and dues that would sap my time and resources while not producing a viable income.

When I walked into Paul's office, he jumped to his feet and shook my hand. "Have a seat, Jim, and thanks for coming in. The more I think about it, the more I think you ought to give this a try. There's more going for property sales up there than you think, and I believe you're the right man for the job."

"No, Paul. I appreciate your confidence in me, but I'm really not interested."

---

23. For more of our story, see my books *Escape to God* and *Come to the Quiet*.

I thought he would drop it, but he didn't. He pressed further, "Jim, I don't think you understand what you're refusing." He proceeded to outline the potential he saw in that remote market. I was about ready to walk out of his office when I sensed that God was trying to tell me something. *"Jim, listen to this man's offer."*

I suddenly realized that God might be trying to answer my prayers and that I was resisting Him, not listening, and being the preeminent one. So I stayed in my seat.

"Jim, what would it take for you to consider conducting real estate sales out of your log cabin in the North Fork valley?"

I took a deep breath and then laid out five conditions that I knew no sane businessman would accept.

"Well, Paul, first of all, you would need to cover all my expenses including advertising and monthly fees."

"No problem, Jim. What else?"

"There are to be no expectations or quotas of any kind. I must not ever be required to attend any meetings. And I can work when I want to and take off when I want to for as long as I want."

"We can do that. Anything else?"

"Um, you will provide a radio phone for me and pay the bill for it." (There was no phone service available to our wilderness home.)

I expected Paul to politely end the conversation, but instead he said, "Anything else?"

I could think of no other objections, so I replied, "No."

He smiled, reached into his desk, pulled out the national and state real estate study exams, handed them to me, and said, "Well, then, let's get started!"

That conversation marked the beginning of a mutually beneficial relationship that lasted for years. I became the number one grossing agent in the company, which allowed me to get on my feet financially and helped prepare me to move into full-time ministry for God. When my two boys came of age, they were both offered the same arrangement and have done very well.

My life has been a process of discovery—discovering how God works and learning to read His divine will through open and closed doors. I have found that this process of discovery requires a humble and open heart. In fact, I have come to see that God is as close as a humbled and open heart.

The day God became real

A friend I'll call Jon owned a thriving real estate development business on the East Coast. While he mentally assented to God's existence, God just wasn't real to him. When he heard me sharing stories about God's interaction with me, he was quietly skeptical.

But that changed a few years ago when Jon faced a financial crisis that was way out of his ability to control or solve. One of his development properties was for sale and a buyer had signed a contract to purchase it. Five days before the anticipated closing date, the buyer decided to back out of the deal and refused to deliver the deposit of one hundred and fifty thousand dollars, even though he admitted it was due Jon.

This unexpected turn of events placed Jon's business in a very difficult position. His company was already severely leveraged and had made business plans contingent on this sale. In fact, this situation put the once-successful business on the verge of bankruptcy.

Jon had never before failed at anything in his life. For the first time, he faced a situation he simply could not handle. I've often seen how God allows us to come to places like this, so that we will finally loosen our grip on having preeminence in our lives. That's what happened with Jon.

He reached out to God like never before. He bargained with God, "Take my arms or legs in an accident. Give me open-heart surgery. Don't let me fail like this. I can't handle it."

As he wrestled with God through the night, all the walls in his heart came down, one at a time. For the first time, he relinquished his veto power to God. He reached a point where he told Jesus that he would love Him unconditionally whether or not his business survived. He told me later that for once, he meant it.

As he continued to wrestle through the long sleepless night, he pleaded with God to have me call him. He felt that my experience as a businessman who also embraced God's principles could help him in this crisis—both with his business and his heart. He didn't really think anything would come of that prayer; we rarely spoke, and he still had a hard time believing that God was active in his life.

Meanwhile, back in Montana, I awakened early as I usually do and headed out the door for my morning run. I was talking with the Lord as I plodded along the forest-lined road when a thought came to my mind: *"Call Jon."*

Hmm, I thought, *I haven't thought of Jon or talked to him in ages.* My thoughts moved on to other things I wanted to pray about.

When I got home, I got in the shower and among steam and soap suds, the thought came again: *"Call Jon."*

"Lord, is that You?" I wondered and then went on with my other thoughts.

At five-thirty I was kneeling by my chair to ask God's blessing and guidance on my reading of His Word when the thought came again: *"Call Jon."*

"Lord, I don't know if You are behind that thought or not, and I apologize for interrupting my quiet time with You this morning, but I've got to call Jon and see what's going on."

I dialed the number, and his wife answered the phone. "Hi, Lorraine! I apologize for calling so early. I don't usually pick up my phone before nine. Is Jon there?"

"Jim? Is this Jim Hohnberger? Oh praise God! Jon has been praying all night that you would call. I'll put him on."

Jon told me later how the tears came to his eyes as he realized that God was a personal God and that He was actively working in his life.

I began the conversation, "So why am I calling you, Jon?"

Jon proceeded to explain the situation and his night of wrestling with God. Our conversation helped to cement his commitment to God at levels one and two. As Jon cooperated with God at these levels, God opened a way for him to face his future dilemma.

God wants to do this for you as well. You can't earn it, but you can untie God's hands by listening with both ears and acting on His guidance.

God calls us to "pray continually."[24] This doesn't mean we don't do anything except pray. Rather, it means that we don't do anything without prayer—two-way communication with God. We keep company with Him at all times.

What would your life be like today if you prayed continually? You would think twice before acting in a harsh way. You would dismiss yourself from an inappropriate conversation or Web site. You would be open to God calling you to guard your eyes, your ears, and your affections. You would become God governed rather than man managed. He—not you—would become the preeminent one!

God is calling to each of us. Why? Why is God calling? Because He wants to walk with us as He did with Enoch.

---

24. 1 Thessalonians 5:17, NIV.

Questions to ponder or discuss with others:

1. Are you like Dennis, with one ear pointed to heaven and your hand cupped around it, saying, "Speak, Lord!" while you have a finger in the other ear?
2. Has God has been convicting you of something that you are refusing to cooperate with Him about?
3. Are you afraid to see yourself as you really are?
4. Is God calling you to "be still and know" His principles in order to adapt your life to His revealed will?
5. When God calls (and He does often), do you listen and follow? Do you want the benefit of His inside information? Or do you dismiss God's call to your heart and conscience?
6. Are you willing to enter into a life of discovery, so that God can reveal His will for your future?
7. Are you ready to untie God's hands by listening with both ears and acting on His guidance?
8. Are you prepared to become God governed rather than man managed?

Chapter 5

"Come, Walk With Me"

*Behold, I stand at the door, and knock: if any man hear my voice,
and open the door, I will come in to him, and will sup with him,
and he with me.*

—Revelation 3:20, KJV

*L*andon and I were playing with Lego bricks in the living room, and we were having a blast! Four-year-old Landon is my oldest grandson and the firstborn of my son Andrew and his wife, Sarah. I have four grandsons and one granddaughter, and I really enjoy them. And they enjoy me! (They call me *Opa,* which is German for "Grandpa.")

When Sally and I had arrived at Landon's house that morning, he was waiting at the door for me. He gave me the tightest hug he could muster and then picked up a box he was just dying to show me.

"What do you have there, Landon?" I asked.

Holding it up for me to see, he burst out, "It's a Lego fire truck, Opa! Will you build it for me?"

"Build it for you? Why don't we build it together?"

"I don't know how."

"Well, I'll show you. We'll do it together. That will be a lot more fun!"

Soon, Landon and I were hunched together on the living room

floor, absorbed in Lego bricks. I showed him how to follow the directions, and he began to catch on. He studied the diagram carefully and then searched through the various shapes, sizes, and colors of Lego pieces to find just the right one. He was so excited to see that fire truck taking shape under his hands! We were searching for the right combination of wheels, when from the kitchen Sally's voice interrupted our concentration.

"Landon, I need you to come help wash the dishes." Sally's voice was sweet but firm. Sally and Sarah were working in the kitchen, and it was Landon's job to help with the dishes when it was needed.

Instantly, Landon's shoulders slumped. He picked up his partly built fire truck and sat there studying it for a moment before answering, "I can't. I'm playing with Opa."

Sally was quick. "Landon, it's your turn to help with the dishes. It won't take long, and then you can play with Opa again."

Landon glanced at me with pleading eyes. I knew he was hoping I would veto Grandma's request. But I didn't intervene.

Landon tried again. "But I don't want to."

Now Sarah stepped in. "Landon, you need to listen to your grandma."

A look of sheer disgust came over his face, but he set down his fire truck and got to his feet. Moaning under his breath, he dragged himself to the kitchen. "Mommy, is life always going to be this way? Will I always have to be under the rulership of older people?"

"Landon, you must choose to do what's right."

"But, Mommy, I don't like it! I was having fun with Opa. Why do I have to do the dishes now? Can't I do them when Opa is not here?"

Taking Landon by the hand, Sarah led him to another room. Sally and I could hear the muffled tones of Sarah reasoning with Landon. We heard Landon arguing a little, and then Sarah leading him in prayer.

A few minutes later, Landon came bouncing out of the back room with his eyes sparkling again. "OK, Grandma, what do you want me to do?" After ten minutes of willing service, he finished the dishes and was back building his fire truck with Opa.

That dusty, narrow old door

As I watched Landon that day, I reflected that he is not unlike you and me. God calls to us multiple times a day. He says, "Behold I stand at *your* door and knock." He wants to come in. He wants to encourage us, help us, guide us, empower us, and save us.

But we're like Landon. "I'm busy!" "I'm playing!" "I'm having fun!" "I don't want to!" Or sometimes we're like the citizens in Jesus' parable who sent a message to the nobleman, saying, "We will not have this man to reign over us."[1] We have an aversion to authority that seems to come to us as a birthright.

There are many things beyond our power to choose—the manner, time, and circumstances of our birth; the condition of the world around us; or the behavior of other people. Considering the experiences that come to us from living in a fallen world, we can feel pretty powerless at times. But there is one choice no one can take from us, regardless of our birth, nationality, social condition, or educational status. We can make the choice to be either man managed or God governed, and God never violates that choice. We can open the door to Him or choose to leave Him out.

God is waiting for His church—you and me—to open that dusty, narrow old door and really let Him in! Yes, many of us have accepted what God has done *for* us. That is the initial opening of the door. But God also comes to us every day and wants to do a work *in* and *through* us. Those are additional doors. Will we hear His voice and open those doors?

The Savior is waiting to enter your heart,
Why don't you let Him come in?
There's nothing in this world to keep you apart,
What is your answer to Him?

Time after time He has waited before,
And now He is waiting again
To see if you're willing
To open the door:
Oh, how He wants to come in. [2]

Veto power

Tammy, a young friend of mine, told me about a conversation she had with her college counselor. He asked her, "If you were God, looking down on you, how would you rate your dedication and wholeheartedness to Him on a scale of one to ten?"

She paused as she weighed the question, and then responded, "Probably an eight." She thought her rating was pretty high, after all, that's 80 percent! That's a lot more than most young people could say. But she was caught off guard when her counselor pursued it further. "What would it take to bring it to a ten?"

1. Luke 19:14.
2. Ralph Carmichael, "The Savior Is Waiting," copyright © 1958 by Sacred Songs.

That question opened up an in-depth discussion about Tammy's hopes and dreams for the future. She is very talented in the field of digital media and has aspirations of making it big in the film industry. She shared her fear that if she gave God absolute and full control of her life, He would restrict her from the things that really matter to her and confine her to a dull, boring existence.

"So you want to retain veto power, don't you?" queried her counselor.

"Yes, I guess I do," she admitted. "I don't mind if God has control over my life as long as I can veto what I don't like."

Tammy, at the age of twenty, was wrestling with the same thing that Landon was struggling with at the age of four—an aversion to authority. Ralph, at the age of forty-five, still had not come to terms with it, either.

Aversion to authority

Sometime ago, I was visiting in a diner with Ralph, an old high-school friend from my days in Appleton, Wisconsin. Ralph and I used to go to wild parties together. Sometimes during recess, we would sneak behind the school to smoke a cigarette. We really thought we were getting away with something—experiencing our "freedom."

As we chatted over lunch, Ralph remarked dryly, "Jim, you sure have changed! You've gotten mighty, uh, religious."

"Oh?" I responded. Ralph didn't seem too positive about the change.

"Do you know why I don't like your religion?"

"No, Ralph, I don't. Please tell me."

Ralph took another bite of his hamburger while studying me seriously. After swallowing, he blurted out, "Because it won't let you do anything anymore. You can't drink alcohol, smoke, swear, party, or watch movies like *Rambo* or *Predator*. You can't even hunt or listen to dirty jokes anymore. Talk about being under the thumb! I wouldn't stand for it. My religion lets me do anything I want. If I want to show up at church, I do. If I don't, I don't. I live a moral life, and that's good enough."

"Really?"

"Yes, really! I don't like anyone telling me what I can or can't do."

It sounded to me like Ralph had a big dose of what my grandson and Tammy were wrestling with. I leaned forward. "Ralph, let me have one of your cigarettes."

"What?" Ralph's expression changed from disgusted to quizzical.

"Just give me a cigarette."

He pulled the packet out of his shirt pocket and handed me a cigarette.

I put the cigarette in my mouth. "Lighter, please."

Now Ralph was totally dumbfounded. He handed me the lighter without a word, and I lit up the cigarette, took a drag on it, blew the smoke in his face, and then snuffed the cigarette out in the nearby ashtray. Looking him in the eye, I said, "There, Ralph. I can choose to smoke or not to smoke. However, you can't choose to *not* smoke. It owns you. I have freedom; you're in bondage."

Ralph scowled at me and took another bite of his hamburger. He was wrestling with an aversion to authority—just like Landon and Tammy did, just like Adam and Eve did back there in the Garden, and just like Lucifer did in heaven. The only difference between Ralph and me is that he's chosen to hold on to his veto power over the call of God to his conscience.

Since that day at the diner, Ralph and I have both grown older under the authority we have each chosen. At the age of sixty-one, I still run three or four miles a day, climb peaks with my son, and feel on top of the world. This last summer, Andrew and I hiked twenty miles round-trip to the summit of Mount Jackson (10,052 feet) in Glacier National Park—all in one day.

Ralph, on the other hand, can't walk to his car without being seriously out of breath. His "freedom" is killing him. My freedom is enabling me. Which would you say has the better management program? Which is the better way of life?

You see, there are benefits to having a Companion who is an expert Authority in all aspects of our lives—not just in the area of health, but also in everything that concerns us. He's an all-encompassing, all-inclusive Coach who's walked the walk before us and has a perfect track record. There is liberty in yielding our veto power to God and listening to His call upon our hearts.

Ralph is choosing to ignore God's voice to his conscience. He's leaving the door closed, and he's paying the price. You see, there is a "high cost to low living." I know, because I paid that price for years before I opened the door to God. It resulted in

- a stale marriage,
- poor health,
- unruly children,
- superficial friendships,
- a guilty conscience,
- outward success at the expense of inward depth of character,
- complacency in place of direction and purpose,
- and being "in the know" instead of an intimate fellowship with the Lord.

Outlaw Inn

Roy was tired of the high cost of low living, which is simply not listening to God. He had kept that dusty, narrow old door closed. He had exercised his veto power and had held on to his aversion to God's authority for too long. His life had become a nauseating mess. Now he was holed up in a dinky room in the Outlaw Inn—a name that was a little too appropriate! His wife had filed for separation; his children wouldn't speak to him; his health was broken; his finances were depleted; and his conscience was tortured with guilt and despair. His life had become a hollow shell.

It's amazing to me how long so many of us resist God. We run from Him, squirm and wiggle our way around Him. We try everything we can think of to make life work the way we want it to, all the while resisting the One who gave us life in the first place and designed its operation. But God doesn't give up on us! He waits for His time and opportunity, continuing to knock on all of our doors. There is no danger that He will give up on us, but there is a great danger in delaying to open the door. We become so used to tuning out His call to our hearts that it becomes increasingly difficult to discern it. If our lives end and we have put off laying down our veto power, we have decided our own fates, and God respects our choices.

In his late fifties, Roy eventually made the choice to lay down his veto power, to open that door, to stop resisting God, and to welcome His authority over his life. When he did that, God was able to teach Roy, situation by situation, how to make his wife a priority and how to invest in his family instead of demanding his own way. Roy's life began to improve. Instead of blaming circumstances and others for his unhappiness, he began to take responsibility for his own thoughts and feelings and the influence he projected. He learned to enter into the hearts of his loved ones instead of continually wounding their spirits. As his attitudes changed, his wife and children were drawn to him instead of dreading his presence. Eventually, he moved back home. Today, Roy has a happy, functioning marriage and family. That's learning to walk with God.

Come and sup

"If any man hear my voice, and open the door, I will come in to him, and will sup with him, and he with me."[3]

The word *sup* is an old English word that we don't typically use in modern conversation, but I like it. To me, it conjures up a warm feeling of connecting with a loved one over a simple, but well-prepared, delicious meal. There's eye contact, energy, interaction, heart, vulnerability, laughter, and tears—real honest connecting. That's what I call "supping"—and that's what our Savior wants

---

3. Revelation 3:20, KJV.

to share with us. He wants fellowship. He sees the future, the present, and our past. He wants to enter into our joys and our sorrows, our fears and our struggles. He wants to share His heart with us. There's no better Counselor, Coach, and Friend. His advice is free, but we have to ask. We have to be willing to *sup* with Him—to hear His voice and respond.

Too often we're reluctant to open the door, because we have subconsciously bought into the devil's propaganda about the One who is knocking. Some see Him as a cold, critical killjoy, while others think of Him as a sappy sugar daddy that can't be taken too seriously. Others are afraid that He's like the important people they have trusted who have let them down. Whatever our misperceptions of God, His Word reveals Him as He truly is, and as we trust Him, He will demonstrate His trustworthiness.

Not complicated

Walking with God is not complicated, but it *seems* hard because we have to interrupt the automatic responses we have all learned to carry in our packs. It's actually simple—very simple. In fact, it can be defined in one sentence. Are you ready for it?

> You need only to cultivate a sense of God's presence with you throughout the day, and then you must be motivated to act on His guidance.

That's it in a nutshell! Simple, isn't it? Learning to recognize God knocking on our door is something we can learn, regardless of our age or place in life. You see, walking with God is an *attitude* and *disposition* of the mind.[4] Your mind surrenders to the habit of listening to His voice[5] and following His guidance according to His Word,[6] and then you pursue this disposition as a way of life.[7] Situation by situation, in small matters as well as the large ones, from the moment you awake until your head hits the pillow at night, you open the door and invite God to sup with you.

You may think that walking with God is an experience reserved for unusual people, but it is not. God specializes in walking with ordinary people and transforming their experiences from ordinary to extraordinary. Let me share a few examples with you.

---

4. See Philippians 2:5.
5. See John 10:27.
6. See Isaiah 8:20.
7. See John 15:4–9.

A listening heart

David is an attorney who knows how to quickly master a situation with his words. That's great if you're his client and he's negotiating on your behalf. It's not always so great if you're the one stepping on his toes. But David is learning to walk with God.

One morning as David was having his devotions, he came across a verse from King Solomon's prayer: "Therefore give to Your servant an understanding heart."[8] A note in the margin defined *understanding* as "hearing." The thought struck a chord in David's mind.

"Lord," he prayed, "please give me a listening heart that I may be hypersensitive to Your calls to me throughout the day."

Later that morning, Gary, his six-year-old son, was helping him feed their four cats—a job Gary loves to do! In fact, he loves it so much that he gets a bit excited and anxious and often makes a mess, scattering cat food on the floor between the storage area and the feeding area.

"Be careful not to spill the food," David had just cautioned when the fully loaded bowl of cat food slipped out of Gary's hands and dumped all over the freshly cleaned hardwood floor.

In a flash, David's prosecuting instincts fired into action, and he opened his mouth to give Gary a sound scolding. But just as quickly, the Holy Spirit called to him to be silent. For one of the first times in his life, he instantly cooperated. He paused for a moment and then said to his crestfallen little boy, "That's OK, Gary. I'll get the broom, and we'll clean this up together."

David didn't realize it, but Cindy, his wife, was watching the whole event as it happened. Later, she told David that when Gary spilled the food, she was about to warn her husband from saying something that would wound Gary's little spirit, but she didn't have to. David didn't just spend time with God in the morning and then go about his man-managed way. He supped with God throughout the day—continuously.

Another way of saying it is that God is the Fountain of life,[9] and He longs to open up within you and me "a fountain of water springing up into everlasting life."[10] He wants to be within us a continuous supply of life, wisdom, and power.[11] He is as available to us as the air we breathe. He longs to be our Alpha and Omega and everything in between—so that we can experience real life. Everyone born on this planet experiences existence, but few enter into life

---

8. 1 Kings 3:9.

9. See Psalm 36:9; Jeremiah 2:13; John 4:10.

10. John 4:14.

11. See John 15:4, 5.

because few open the door to the Life-Giver.

Instead, we treat God like a water fountain. When we feel thirsty, we go get a drink, quench our thirst, and then go our merry way until the need arises again. This on-again off-again experience robs us of the true joy and fulfillment God intends for us.

But we may open the door and let Him in—and then this Fountain of sweet water can flow within us, continuously, even when our son dumps the cat food on the floor. "He who has the Son has life; he who does not have the Son of God does not have life."[12] David is finding a listening heart; he is becoming "swift to hear, slow to speak, slow to wrath."[13] He's discovering that a listening heart is the passport to peace, happiness, and joy.

God directing

Steve is a government employee. Often, his work requires him to travel to different towns for meetings and inspections. Usually, one of his colleagues travels with him, and they either discuss work-related business or listen to the local radio station. When Steve travels alone, he listens to a sermon or Christian music.

One particular day, as Steve got in the car with his colleague, Scott, he was impressed to play one of my sermons from the *Escape to God* album. *Lord, is that You? I can't play that. This man is from a different religion than mine, and he might get offended or think I'm trying to convert him or something. After all, he's a captive audience and has no place to go.*

"Steve, are you embarrassed about Me? Are you willing to take a risk of being misunderstood for My sake?"

Steve pondered for a moment and then turned to Scott. "Scott, I usually listen to some sort of sermon while I drive. Would you mind if I put one on today?"

Scott shook his head and said, "No problem. Go for it!"

Steve popped in the CD, and they were on their way. An hour later, they arrived at their destination, and the message ended. Scott exclaimed, "Wow! That was great! I really enjoyed that. Could I borrow the CD to share with my family?"

Steve just happened to have the complete *Escape to God* album with him, and he gladly gave it to Scott.

A few days later, they were driving together again, and this time Steve felt more courageous. "Hey Scott, what can I indoctrinate you with this time?"

Scott chuckled. "Play whatever you want. If it's as good as what you shared last time, I'm all ears."

---

12. 1 John 5:12.
13. James 1:19.

Steve sent up a silent prayer and was impressed to put on a message about health. Scott liked it and asked to borrow it too. At the end of the trip, as Scott was walking away from the car, he commented, "Thanks again for those *Escape to God* CDs. They are changing the way we think about family and are bringing us closer to each other."

Steve is finding the key to success—a God-directed life in all situations. He's discovering that saying Yes to God is opening new horizons and solving old dilemmas.

A principled life

George lived in a rural community in South Africa where his office was located and traveled frequently to the various towns that he managed. As George traveled, he listened to *Escape to God, Back to the Basics, Come Up Higher,*[14] and other similar messages. At home, Sandy and his three children kept the TV playing and watched the sitcoms and "soaps" that came on every afternoon. George joined them when he got home from work early enough.

When Three Angels' Broadcasting Network and Hope Channel started broadcasting in Africa, George was impressed to install a satellite dish and decoder at his home—a rather large expense. Then he and his family watched the Christian channels on Sabbath and all the other nonreligious stuff during the rest of the week.

His daughter, Rachel, had just graduated from elementary school and was facing leaving home to go to boarding school. Neither Rachel nor Sandy were comfortable with the idea of Rachel living in the dormitory. Sandy decided that it would be wise to move near Rachel's new school, so that she could attend school from home. They went house hunting and found an affordable house large enough to accommodate their needs.

Sandy and the children moved to the city, while George planned to stay in the rural town near his office during the week until he could arrange a transfer to an office in the city. George loaded up the furniture and belongings his family would need at the new house. As he was getting ready to load up the TV, a thought whispered in his mind: *"Don't take the TV to the city. Leave it here and leave it turned off."*

"Lord, my family won't be very happy with me if I don't take them the TV."

"George, give them some time to get used to not having the TV, so that they will find the joy of talking to each other again and not rushing through worship to tune in to the next episode of some program."

When George unloaded the truck at the new house, his family quickly

---

14. All of these CD seminars are available from Empowered Living Ministries.

noticed that he had not brought the TV. "Hey, Dad, where's the TV?" his son asked.

"Oh, I didn't bring it. When I have time to install the satellite dish and decoder here, I'll bring it down."

Sandy overheard what he was saying, and a look of irritation came over her face. "George, we always watch TV. What are we supposed to do all evening without it?"

George gave her a sympathetic smile while sending up a silent prayer to God. Then he simply said, "Talk to each other."

This was greeted with a cry of protest from his whole family. In fact, the grumbling continued for several months—whenever George was home. He was sorely tempted to bring the TV and hook it up just to quell the discontent.

But God kept whispering to his mind: *"Don't give in, George. Leave it far away from them until they get used to not having it all the time."* George was learning to recognize God's still, small Voice to his conscience. He believed this was God calling to him because it was not in harmony with his own thoughts and desires. But it was in harmony with the principles of God's Word that George was contemplating while he drove around in his car and conversed with God.[15]

In spite of the conflict, George listened to God. In time, he was able to transfer from the rural office to an office in the city and stay with his family. Without the distraction of the TV, they were able to start regular family worship morning and evening. In the evenings, they had time to talk with each other before the kids went to bed or to their rooms to study. The children shared what was happening at school, and George and Sandy entered into their concerns and were able to share guidelines to help them successfully work through their difficulties.

After about six months, George and his family were adjusting to the new routine. Pleasant conversation had replaced the grumbling, and no one seemed to miss the TV anymore. "Lord, is it time to hook up the satellite for 3ABN?"

"Wait just a little longer."

After another two months, George brought the TV set to their new home and set it up to receive only 3ABN. He did not install the external antenna to receive the local TV channels. He wondered if anyone would complain. But they did not. They had become so used to not watching that having the TV there did not bother them. In fact, they preferred to leave it off because they had learned to value the peace and quiet of home over the babble of TV programming.

---

15. See Philippians 4:8.

Another benefit was that the children's school performance improved. They had more time to study and to talk through their difficulties with their parents. The family ate all their meals together at the table and enjoyed interacting with each other.

One evening, Rachel asked George if they could go for a father-daughter walk. As they started down the lane, Rachel slipped her hand in her daddy's hand and said, "Father, I've been wanting to tell you something."

Glancing at her, George replied, "What's on your mind, sweetheart?"

"Well, you remember how we complained when you didn't bring the TV to our new house right away?"

George nodded.

"I really resented that for a while. But now I can see why you did it. Our family is so much closer now. Our worship times and talk times have become my favorite part of the day, and I think we are growing more in Christ. I just wanted to say Thank you!"

George is learning that a principled life based on God's Word and God's direction is the best life for all. It's transforming his marriage, family, and everyday life.

He cares for you!

Hans is a friend of mine from another country. He has distinguished himself in corporate sales for more than twenty years. He had been a Christian for just a short time when he decided to leave a very lucrative sales position that was, as he put it, "destroying my life." He opted for a quieter, less stressful position with little chance for promotion or earning a major income. He was happy and content because his new position allowed him time to pursue his growing relationship with Christ and to share that relationship with others.

One day, he was approached by one of the senior managers of the company he worked for. He wanted to know if Hans would be interested in a manager's position in sales. This gentleman was well acquainted with Hans's experience and expertise, and Hans knew that he would not be approaching him in this way if he had not already been "earmarked" for the position. He also knew that you don't say No to this kind of offer. A very strong, though unspoken, expectation is that you accept the position if it is offered to you.

The old man-managed Hans, who was driven by ego and success, wanted to jump at the opportunity. In fact, that's just what the company wanted. Large corporations prey on a person's sense of having to achieve in order to be somebody. Hans's wife wanted him to accept the position because it would mean he would not have to travel so far to work—the position was close to home. Various senior officials made very friendly approaches and let him know he was their top pick for the position and how wonderful it would be for him when he accepted. Everyone was sure he would accept it—everyone, that is, but Hans.

You see, Hans had opened the door to Christ and knew what it meant to sup with Him. Before he knew God, his life had been centered on his own self-fulfillment. He would have gone for the interview, landed the job, and then negotiated for the salary and benefits. Since management had approached him, he assumed that a good salary increase would be part of the package he would be offered.

But Hans was learning to listen to God's voice. So he went to his knees and put the decision in God's hands. As he opened up the situation to God, a single sentence was impressed on his mind: *"Look, and ask what they* cannot *give."*

He wondered, *Is this the voice of the Holy Spirit to my conscience?* He had heard this whispering in his conscience when he had found God nearly a year earlier, as well as a number of times since. He had also had the experience of choosing to ignore what he heard and found that the situation usually escalated into a bad one.

But he wondered, *What does this mean? Why ask for something they cannot give?*

As he pondered what this meant and how to proceed, he received a daily devotional via e-mail that quoted Isaiah 1:10, "Jerusalem, your rulers and your people are like those of Sodom and Gomorrah. *Listen* to what the Lord is saying to you. *Pay attention* to what our God is teaching you" (TEV; emphasis added).

But what is He teaching me? Hans wondered. *If I accept the position, everyone will be happy with me. What is God trying to say? It doesn't seem clear.*

Then another e-mail popped into his inbox. It was from another senior manager who wanted to know Hans's decision. This manager had accidentally forgotten to delete another message at the bottom of the e-mail—a message that Hans was not supposed to see. It stated what the salary was to be for the position Hans was being offered—and the salary was considerably less than Hans was already earning.

The light came on for Hans. God was clearly warning him to proceed with caution. So Hans sent a respectful e-mail to the person offering him the job, specifying two conditions: First, he must continue to have Sabbaths off from work. Second, he asked for a reasonable salary increase based on the salary scale of the position offered.

The response surprised Hans a bit. Management was prepared to accommodate the Sabbath request, but they said his salary expectation was "unrealistic." They told him that he would save a lot of money by reducing his travel expenses and that the prestige of the job actually warranted a *decrease* in salary.

He declined the offer. Then he discovered that his senior manager had already been told that Hans was going to accept the job. The manager phoned Hans directly, and Hans was able to share with him how God had guided him. Hans's manager told him off the record that it was the right decision. In fact, if Hans had formally applied for the position, he would have been virtually forced into it.

A lot of people were initially upset with Hans's decision, but Hans was at rest. He knew that God had protected him from an unwise step. Though he has been a Christian only for one year, Hans is tasting the benefits of cultivating a sense of God's presence and then acting on His counsel. This attitude and disposition is charting a safe course through the unknown mazes of life.

Learning to walk

Let's review. So many of us begin life like my four-year-old grandson Landon—wanting total control over the reins of our lives. As we grow into adulthood, we may find a moral life or even a religious life, but, like Tammy, we let God have only 80 percent of us. We retain our veto power in select areas of our lives. Or we may cherish a complete aversion to authority like Ralph did, whether that aversion is to the authority of a church, God's Word, or God Himself speaking to our conscience. To our own detriment, we defiantly live life "our way."

Some of us wind up at the Outlaw Inn, with only a hollow shell of life left and finally find the motivation to open the door to God. Then we discover that God was there all the time—not as an adversary, but as an Advocate—wanting to sup and walk with us daily. A listening heart is awakened, and we discover that all we need to do is cultivate a sense of God's presence with us throughout our day and then act on His guidance. We experience God directing our lives for witnessing, for principled living, and for our future welfare. We come to find out that He cares for us in all the details of everyday living. This learning to walk with God entails exchanging our old habit patterns for new ones. It means that the old man-managed ways are replaced with a God-governed life. It begins by learning to habituate our hearts, minds, and consciences to the whisperings of God according to His Word—one choice at a time. Choices that are often repeated build new habits and patterns. Repeated habits and patterns form a new character. This is how we learn to walk with God, daily, hourly, day-in and day-out.

Does this mean we'll live a utopian life with no problems or difficulties? Not if the devil has anything to say about it! As sure as you or I begin to find this new life in Jesus, the devil sets about to distract, discourage, and drown us in trouble.

Questions to ponder or discuss with others:

1. When God calls, do you reply, like Landon, "I'm busy; I'm playing; I'm having fun; I don't want to"?
2. Do you have an aversion to rightful authority?
3. Are you man managed or God governed?
4. Do you want to retain veto power over God's direction in your life?
5. Do you have true freedom or are you in bondage to your habits?
6. Are you paying the high cost of low living?
7. Is God knocking on your door right now? What is He asking?
8. Do you think that walking with God is an experience reserved only for "unusual people"?
9. Do you possess a "listening heart"? All the time? Some of the time? Almost never?
10. Are you determined to begin recognizing God as your daily Advocate?

Chapter 6

Drowning in Trouble

I stretch forth my hands unto thee. . . . For in thee do I trust.
—Psalm 143:6, 8, KJV

ave you seen the movie *Flywheel*? A friend mailed me a copy of the DVD, saying, "You've got to watch this!" I did, and I really enjoyed the movie. It's a great story! I can enter into the mind-set of the man-managed individual running his business, using all the shrewdness of corporate America to make a profit. I feel his frustration as his business runs into the ground and his life falls apart. My tears flow as he gives himself to God and everything turns around. God saves his business; his wife is in love with him again; he becomes his son's hero; and he ends up featured on TV as an icon of virtue. Then my indignation rises as he faces some frenemy fire, but God brings people to vindicate him. His wife gives birth to a beautiful baby girl, and he lives happily ever after.

I love the story, but it leaves a big question mark in my mind. Does following God mean I will have a trouble-free life? It's true that the benefits of walking with God are real and tangible, but does the gospel create a bubble of nirvana in which every problem is resolved to my benefit? I don't think so. If you're not sure about that, ask Job. Ask David, Joseph, Elisha, Paul, and others. They all faced serious difficulties in spite of the fact that they honestly lived for God.

So what do you do when you find yourself drowning in trouble? What's next?

Facing foreclosure

My oldest son, Matthew, is a real estate broker. One day, he called me on the phone. "Father, why don't you join me to look at a couple of country homes. I'd like to see what you think of them for my family."

We pulled up to a quaint, cedar-log home situated among fragrant evergreens. The manicured lawn, sprawling picnic table, and graceful shrubs presented a vision of loveliness. A large, insulated two-car garage with a carport on each side, sat to the left of the house. A pleasant couple, who appeared to be in their fifties, met us at the front door. As we entered the home, it was obvious that they had really thrown their time, talents, and hearts into this place.

"You really have a nice place here," Matthew began. "Why do you want to sell it?"

I noticed that the wife kind of winced and looked down. Her husband answered, "Well, actually, we really don't want to sell it. This is our dream home. Starting with a bare piece of land fifteen years ago, we have built most of it ourselves. But with this present economy, my employer has reduced my work hours, and we simply can't make the payments. The bank has scheduled foreclosure in sixty days."

"Oh, that's too bad!" Matthew sympathized. "What will you do?"

"Start over again, I guess. That's our only option."

My heart ached for them. I noticed a Bible and a book about Jesus on a table, and I wondered, *Has God forsaken them? Does He not hear their prayers? Doesn't He care that they are losing almost all their equity? Is it because of some great sin in their life that He refuses to comfort them and work in their behalf?*

Startled, scared, and confused

"Jim, I need your advice about my marriage." Amy's voice over the phone sounded strained. "Dave put a gun to my head last night and threatened to pull the trigger."

"Oh, my!" I exclaimed. "Has he ever done that before?"

At one of my meetings, Dave and Amy had come to me, asking for help with the struggles in their marriage. I had helped them form a solution-oriented plan based on God's principles, and they had been working the plan. The last time I had talked with them, they were doing much better. Amy brought me up-to-date.

"No, Dave has never done anything like this before. This is totally out of character for him. He's been under a lot of stress lately. It's getting harder and harder for him to find work and pay our bills. Working long, hard hours at two different jobs doesn't leave him enough time to relax, and so he doesn't sleep well.

"Last evening, he came home exhausted. I brought up a problem that I'm having with one of the children. I had put off talking to him about it because I know he's stretched to the max. But last night I really felt like I needed his input. But when I brought it up, he said, 'Not now, Amy. I can't deal with this.'

"I know I should have let it go, but I didn't. I pressed him. He told me he couldn't take any more negative stuff.

"I said, 'That's not an excuse.' He left the room and shut the door. I followed him and pressed him further.

"That's when he blew. He pulled a gun out of the dresser, put it to my head, and told me to stop—or else."

So, what about Dave and Amy? Can their marriage work? Can God restore their brokenness? Why does God seem so distant to so many couples? Has the gospel lost its power to save unto the uttermost?

Devastated

Ron and Ann were devastated. Their good friends of nearly ten years had turned on them in an ugly series of misunderstandings. Ron and Ann tried to clarify things, but the harder they tried, the greater the distance became. The situation was turning into a quagmire.

Now they started hearing reports from other people of the innuendos and half-truths that were being spread about them. It seemed that their former friends were purposely trying to discredit them, so that others would view them as two-faced hypocrites.

Why? How can two couples, who have been friends for almost a decade, turn on each other? They went to the same church, were involved in the same mission projects, vacationed together, faced character issues together, and helped each other grow in their walk with God. They had vowed they'd be "forever friends." Now this!

What are Ron and Ann supposed to do? Do they retaliate? Fight fire with fire? Roll over and play dead? Where is God in all this? Why doesn't He protect them from these sick attacks? Doesn't He care about their reputation? Is this how Christian friends behave? Why does God allow them to still play church, put on a face, and appear so pious? Why doesn't He expose evil while protecting and shielding the innocent?

"Deliver me, O Lord!"

If you feel like you are drowning in trouble, it may be a sign that you are doing something right. If you are honestly dealing with that pack of preeminence on your back, responding to God's call to your heart, and opening that dusty, narrow old door, Satan will erect mountains of frightful conditions before you to drive you to unbelief and despair. He is a master at distracting us with detours. He floods us with doubts and fears—some of which may have never crossed our minds before. His strategy is to turn our focus onto the question of how bad are things going to get, rather than onto God's promises to keep us through the bad times!

What are you facing? Unemployment? Foreclosure? A serious health crisis? Strained family relationships? Marital stress or divorce? Accidents? Financial woe? Fumbled friendships? Tension on the job? Religious opposition or intolerance? What would you add to the list?

Can you identify with the sinking feeling that threatens to drown your courage and faith? Do you find yourself asking, Where, oh where, is God in all this? David asked that question, and his life is a lighthouse of encouragement for all of us who are overwhelmed with difficulties. Although God seemed to delay relief, David learned to seek Him, to lean on Him, and to cry out in his pain and confusion. Just read Psalm 143.

Hear my prayer, O Lord,
Give ear to my supplications!
In Your faithfulness answer me,
And in Your righteousness.
Do not enter into judgment with Your servant,
For in Your sight no one living is righteous.

For the enemy has persecuted my soul;
He has crushed my life to the ground;
He has made me dwell in darkness,
Like those who have long been dead.
Therefore my spirit is overwhelmed within me;
My heart within me is distressed.

I remember the days of old;
I meditate on all Your works;
I muse on the work of Your hands.
I spread out my hands to You;
My soul longs for You like a thirsty land. Selah

Answer me speedily, O LORD;
My spirit fails!
Do not hide Your face from me,
Lest I be like those who go down into the pit.
Cause me to hear Your lovingkindness in the morning,
For in You do I trust;
Cause me to know the way in which I should walk,
For I lift up my soul to You.

Deliver me, O LORD, from my enemies;
In You I take shelter.
Teach me to do Your will,
For You are my God;
Your Spirit is good.
Lead me in the land of uprightness.

Revive me, O LORD, for Your name's sake!
For Your righteousness' sake bring my soul out of trouble.
In Your mercy cut off my enemies,
And destroy all those who afflict my soul;
For I am Your servant.

God had everything under control in David's life, but it sure didn't feel like it to David as he fled from the maniacal King Saul and huddled in the caves of the wilderness. Still, feelings or no feelings, David held on to God, and God saw him through.

God has everything under control in your life as well! Do you believe that? If you will trust Him as David did, God will take you through all the days ahead.

Joseph didn't have things too easy, either, but he did not close the door on God. Sold into slavery by his own brothers, rewarded with jail time for his faithful service to Potiphar, Joseph was unswerving in his purpose to honor and trust God to the end. Through all those years of cruel bondage, Joseph did not lose his hold on God.

Imagine what it would have been like to be in Paul's shoes. Everywhere he went, bearing the good news of God's grace, he met opposition, and that opposition was a lot more serious than mere disagreement. For instance, in Lystra, the people were ready to worship him as a Greek god, and moments later, they dragged him out of the city, stoned him, and left him for dead! Did Paul put his tail between his legs and run for home? No! He wrote, "I consider that the sufferings of this present time are not worthy to be compared with the glory which shall be revealed in us."[1]

The most obvious biblical example of drowning in trouble is Job. Job had it all, and in one short period of time, he lost it all—even his health. His wife turned her contempt on God and egged Job on to do the same. His well-meaning, but misguided friends dumped guilt on Job for his sudden reverses. Job suffered grief, loneliness, and depression. He even wished he could die or had never been born. Yet in the midst of it all, he clung tenaciously to God. He cried out, "Though He slay me, yet will I trust Him."[2]

The devil may engineer circumstances to strip you of your possessions, undermine your relationships, weaken your health, or blacken your reputation, but he can never touch the life that is hid with Christ in God. As long as we take refuge in Him, we are secure.

The eyes of faith

Elisha took refuge in that secret place. During a Syrian invasion of Israel, the king of Syria decided to capture Elisha because he was reporting to the king of Israel the plans of the enemy. Every time the Syrian king laid an ambush for the Israelite king, God would forewarn Elisha, who would forewarn the Israelite king and thus foil the Syrian plot.

After a while, the king of Syria got tired of the misfiring operations and decided to take out Elisha. Spies reported Elisha's location, and the Syrian king dispatched a regiment of "horses and chariots and a great army there, and they came by night and surrounded the city. And when the servant of the man of God arose early and went out, there was an army, surrounding the city with horses and chariots."[3]

Elisha's servant was terrified. He immediately knew that he and Elisha were outnumbered, outmaneuvered, and without visible help. He ran to Elisha exclaiming, "Alas, my master! What shall we do?"[4]

Elisha didn't flinch. Instead, he replied calmly, "Do not fear, for those who are with us are more than those who are with them." As Elisha's servant gawked at him in disbelief, "Elisha prayed, and said, 'LORD, I pray, open his eyes that he may see.' Then the LORD opened the eyes of the young man, and he saw. And behold, the mountain was full of horses and chariots of fire all around Elisha."[5]

---

1. Romans 8:18.
2. Job 13:15.
3. 2 Kings 6:14, 15.
4. 2 Kings 6:15.
5. 2 Kings 6:16, 17.

Elisha saw with the eyes of faith that "greater is he that is in you, than he that is in the world."[6] The chariots of God far surpassed those of the Syrian army, but they were discerned only with the eyes of faith—a faith that puts more weight on the promises of God than on the threats of our dark circumstances. Who are you: Elisha or his servant?

The secret place

The secret place is where faith in God becomes a greater reality than our circumstances! We can read about it in Psalm 91:

> He who dwells in the secret place of the Most High

The secret place is the freedom to choose which reality we will live in—the seen or the unseen. Real Christian life is 10 percent what happens to us, and 90 percent how we respond to it. We often find a chasm between the seen and the unseen worlds—much like Elisha's servant did. Faith bridges the gap! Faith sees God's ability to save and deliver. Faith sees our disasters as God's opportunities to reveal His will to us. Faith sees the evidence of God's work in our lives.

Through active faith, we can turn off the constant negative tapes that play in our heads so easily. By faith, we can say, "I have put my life in the Lord's hands. 'I know whom I have believed and am persuaded that He is able to keep what I have committed to Him until that Day.' "[7] God will faithfully keep His word to preserve us *through* the pain, sorrow, and disappointments.

To dwell in that secret place means to stay there, to take up permanent residence. "Come what may, I'm not leaving, Lord! You are my reality—not my circumstances!" That's entering into a real faith experience!

> Shall abide under the shadow of the Almighty.

He is El Shaddai—the all-sufficient One. He speaks, and worlds swirl into existence.[8] He is constantly aware of everything happening in the universe—from the smallest subatomic particle to the largest heavenly galaxy.[9] He knows

---

6. 1 John 4:4, KJV.
7. 2 Timothy 1:12.
8. See Psalm 33:9.
9. Isaiah 40:28.

how many hairs are on your head,[10] and He marks every tear and smile that crosses your face.[11] You will not trust Him in vain.[12] Do you believe that? Is that your reality? Just look at David's attitude!

I will say of the LORD, "He is . . .

Notice the word *is*. That's a present tense, state-of-being verb. It reminds me of what Paul said in Hebrews 11:6. "He who comes to God must believe that *He is,* and that He is a rewarder of those who diligently seek Him" (emphasis added). That describes David's faith. It was present tense—ongoing—happening. He believed that God was personal, present, and active in his life for His own loving purposes.[13]

"my refuge and my fortress;

David dwelt in God—not in his troubles and sorrows, disappointments and discouragements.

"My God, in Him I will trust."

God is personal and present. I'm familiar with Him. He's my constant Companion. "In Him will I trust"—not in my finances or the economy, not in my self-sufficient lifestyle, not in my church or good works or distinctive understanding of truth, and not in my health or circumstances. No! Like David, Joseph, Job, Paul, and Elisha, I will affirm, "In Him will I trust!" This is the currency of life. This is the common thread that God wants to weave through all our troubles.

He wants to lead us all into an experience of utter dependence on Him. This is what we have the opportunity to gain. Whether it's through the loss of your home, livelihood, marriage, friendships, health, or family, God is at work through these circumstances to draw you into utter dependence on Him. As these troubles gather about us, our choice is clear. We are to resign ourselves into the Lord's hands and actively trust in Him.

Surely He shall deliver you from the snare of the fowler

---

10. See Matthew 10:30.
11. See Psalm 34:15.
12. See Isaiah 45:19.
13. Hebrews 11:6.

And from the perilous pestilence.
He shall cover you with His feathers,
And under His wings you shall take refuge;
His truth shall be your shield and buckler.
You shall not be afraid of the terror by night,
Nor of the arrow that flies by day,
Nor of the pestilence that walks in darkness,
Nor of the destruction that lays waste at noonday.

A thousand may fall at your side,
And ten thousand at your right hand;
But it shall not come near you.
Only with your eyes shall you look,
And see the reward of the wicked.

David is talking about some serious trouble. Any one of these things is a tough pill to swallow. But in God's hands, they become God's medicine. He preserves us through them just as He did Shadrach, Meshach, and Abed-Nego in the fire. Only the cords that bound them were consumed. He wants to be with us in our fire!

Because you have made the LORD, who is my refuge,
Even the Most High, your dwelling place,
No evil shall befall you,
Nor shall any plague come near your dwelling;

At first glance, it sounds like David is saying that God's people won't ever be flooded with trouble, but that was not David's reality—and it's not God's agenda. Look a little closer at these verses. Where is your dwelling? If you are dwelling in the "secret place"—in God—all the muck that the devil throws at you can't take you out of it. You are secure.

When God says, "No evil shall befall you," He is not saying that we won't experience the pain and devastation that evil inflicts on us. Jesus said, "Fear not them which kill the body, but are not able to kill the soul: but rather fear him which is able to destroy both soul and body in hell."[14] Don't fear the economy that is able to destroy your financial security; don't fear your turncoat friends who are able to tarnish your reputation; don't fear your spouse who is able to make your home a hell. Fear God who holds your eternity in His hands. Fear

---

14. Matthew 10:28, KJV.

that you will fail to love Him with every fiber of your being and your neighbor as yourself. God is interested in preserving your soul (character) from evil.[15]

The one thing the devil can never do to a child of God is to infuse evil into his or her soul without his or her permission. But he will do all in his power to entice us to leave the secret place. There is no greater tragedy than for a child of God to let go of his or her trust and pick up the propaganda of the enemy against God. When you cease to " 'love the LORD your God with all your heart, with all your soul, with all your strength, and with all your mind,' and 'your neighbor as yourself,' "[16] evil has befallen you. But as long as you dwell in the secret place, your life is hid with Christ in God, and no one can pluck you out of His hands.[17]

In other words, we must meet our afflictions with a commitment to invest in loving God and others. None of the afflictions of life can rob us of the privilege of being the disciple of Christ. We need not consent to give up the one thing we can hold on to—a life hid with Christ in God.

> For He shall give His angels charge over you,
> To keep you in all your ways.
> In their hands they shall bear you up,
> Lest you dash your foot against a stone.
> You shall tread upon the lion and the cobra,
> The young lion and the serpent you shall trample underfoot.

> "Because he has set his love upon Me, therefore I will deliver him;
> I will set him on high, because he has known My name.
> He shall call upon Me, and I will answer him;
> I will be with him in trouble;
> I will deliver him and honor him.
> With long life I will satisfy him,
> And show him My salvation."

Have you set your love upon God? Are your affections fastened on Him? Is it the focus of your life to know Him—personally, intimately, daily? This is not easy. It requires an active faith. Many things bombard us to knock our focus off Him and onto our problems, to keep us from "the secret place," to cloud the unseen realities with our pressing visible circumstances, to cause us to doubt

---

15. See Psalm 121:7
16. Luke 10:27.
17. See John 10:29.

and despair, to get us to listen to the devil's lies that God will not fight for us, and to make us forget that God is in charge of our life!

Cake recipe

I recently read about a daughter who was telling her mother how everything was going wrong in her life. She was failing algebra. Her boyfriend had broken up with her. And her best friend was moving away.

As she poured out her woes, her mother was mixing the ingredients for a cake. She listened thoughtfully, and when her daughter ran out of complaints, she asked, "Would you like a snack?"

"Absolutely, Mom. I love your cake!"

"Here, then," her mother offered. "Have some cooking oil."

"Yuck!" exclaimed her daughter, turning up her nose.

"How about a couple of raw eggs?"

"Gross, Mom!"

"Would you like some flour then? Or maybe baking soda?"

"Mom, those are all yucky!"

"Yes," her mother replied, "all those things are yucky by themselves. But when they are put together in the right way, they make a wonderfully delicious cake."

God works the same way. Many times we wonder why He would let us go through such difficult times. But God knows that when we trust Him and dwell in the secret place, He will put these things all in His order and cause them to always work for good.[18] You see, that cake represents our character, and God is interested in our lives producing a fragrant, tasty character. As we trust Him, these hard times will eventually produce something wonderful!

Was that true for David? Yes! In spite of being on King Saul's most wanted list for years, David became a man after God's own heart.[19] Was that true for Joseph? Absolutely! The character he developed through his years of grinding bondage prepared him to play a pivotal part in the history of Egypt and Israel. Was it true for Job? Job never understood what was happening behind the scenes of his tragedies, but his faithfulness vindicated God from the accusations the devil had made against him.

How about you and me? Will we let our troubles work for the good that God intends for us?

What makes the difference between being drowned by our difficulties and

---

18. See Romans 8:28.
19. 1 Samuel 13:14.

being delivered through them? It is our choice to dwell in the secret place of the Most High; to resign ourselves into God's care; and to put ourselves completely under His power, wisdom, and mercy! It is allowing His ingredients and His baking time to produce the end result He has in mind. He is "the author and finisher of our faith."[20]

Resist and embrace

We've got to resist the devil's propaganda and embrace the promises of God. That means trusting and cooperating with the Holy Spirit to keep our souls at rest, being convinced that God is working out all things for our good and His overall purpose. It means we are to resist anxiety and embrace calm! It means resting in this declaration from Paul: "We know that all things work together for good to those who love God, to those who are the called according to His purpose."[21]

In other words, circumstances should not dictate our reality. God always has the final word. Clinging by faith to even one promise of God is sufficient to keep you in the secret place. Here are some of my favorite promises:

God is my defense (Psalm 59:9).

The LORD will fight for you, and you shall hold your peace (Exodus 14:14).

My soul, wait silently for God alone,
For my expectation is from Him (Psalm 62:5).

Beloved, I pray that you may prosper in all things and be in health, just as your soul prospers (3 John 2).

We must come to believe that somewhere in our pain, in our never-ending suffering, in the loss of our precious dreams, hopes, and goals, God is taking us deeper in our dependence in Him.

When all of life is going well, it is easy for us to testify, "God can do anything!" We can easily assure others that God will answer their prayers. We can confidently declare that the Lord always keeps His word.

But when everything around us begins to conspire against God's promises being fulfilled, when all the physical evidence seems more like God's wrath than

---

20. Hebrews 12:2.
21. Romans 8:28.

His reward, when it seems that we are the victims rather than the victors, when life seems bitter rather than better—that is the time to hold on! Trust Him! You are not separated from God's love and watchful care. He is at work.

Your cake is being prepared. It might even be in the oven. Don't waver or stagger. Rise up and fight the good fight of faith. Resign yourself totally into God's care. He has everything under control! He will bring you through all that's ahead.

How worried or concerned do you think sheep are as they follow their shepherd through difficult paths into open pastures? They're not worried at all because they're totally resigned to the shepherd's leading. We are the sheep of Christ. He is our Great Shepherd. Why, then, should we be concerned, disquieted, or worried about our lives and future? He knows perfectly how to protect and preserve us.

Then, today, instead of trying to save yourself from drowning in trouble, commit the keeping of your life wholly to God's care—and then rest!

Questions to ponder or discuss with others:

1. Does giving your life fully and completely to Jesus Christ guarantee you a trouble-free existence?
2. Do you focus on how bad things are going to get, rather than keeping your mind on God's promises to help you through the bad times?
3. Do you believe that God has everything under control in your life?
4. Have you lost your hold on God?
5. Like Job, can you cry out, "Though He slay me, yet will I trust Him"?
6. Are you able to discern with the eye of faith—a faith that puts more weight on the promises of God than on the threats of your dark circumstances?
7. By faith, can you turn off the constant negative tapes that play so easily in your head?
8. What defines your reality—God or your state of affairs?
9. Do you believe or understand that through all these adverse circumstances God wants to draw you into utter dependence on Him?
10. Do you know how to dwell in the "secret place"?
11. What makes the difference between being drowned in your difficulties or delivered through them?
12. Do you believe that God always has the final word?

Chapter 7

A Focused Life

Let your eyes look straight ahead,
And your eyelids look right before you.
Ponder the path of your feet,
And let all your ways be established.
Do not turn to the right or to the left.

—Proverbs 4:25–27

When I was running in circles through the world's mazes, one of the things I hated was the continual gnawing reality that my life was not my own. My business owned me. Society owned me. Sports owned me. My hunting and drinking buddies owned me. Church duties and rituals owned me. Keeping up with the Joneses owned me. My bad habits owned me. I felt like a puppet with strings attached to every part of me—strings that kept me dancing to the tune someone else was piping.

I paid a price too! I was stressed, busied, and pushed. I began to experience insomnia. I was easily irritated. My marriage grew stale, and I didn't know my own children. I felt like a disjointed, unbalanced, out-of-control puppet with

only a pretension to the meaningful life I saw promised in the Scriptures. I hungered for authentic Christianity and true purpose.

Was there such a thing as life without the strings? Was it possible to own my own life? Who could cut those strings and set me free? Was there a part I needed to play in the process? Must I always burn myself out, churning through the periphery of life, while the deep realities I wanted to grasp always seemed to elude me? These thoughts and others like them began as whispers in my conscience, and then they swelled louder and louder until I cried out in desperation, "There's got to be a better way!"

That's when the Voice at that dusty, narrow old door called, *"Jim, come to Me. I will give you freedom. Your life need not be controlled by other people, circumstances, or your own carnal nature. When I set you free, you will be free indeed!"*[1]

"But, Lord, I've always thought that when someone surrenders to You, You just pick up those puppet strings and make him dance to Your tune. Isn't that what the surrender of self is all about?"

"No, Jim. Nothing could be further from the truth. If I wanted people to be mere puppets, sin never would have come up in the first place. It's because I created people to be individuals, with the power to think, to do, to purpose, to plan, to love, and to choose, that there was ever the possibility of evil.

"When you take charge of your own life apart from Me, you will always find strings attached that are controlled by a power from beneath, which wants to destroy your life. When you put Me in charge, we become partners to sever those strings and to fulfill the purpose you were created for. You have a place to fill and a work to do that no one else can do, and I will teach you how to accomplish that."[2]

As I considered these things and consulted my conscience, I was led to write in the front cover of my Bible: "Life has taught me that 'things' and getting things done aren't what make up one's life. Life is about walking with God and doing His will day by day."

Life is made up of time. How you spend your time is a reflection of who you are. God has a plan for how you will spend your time, and so does the devil. The devil wants to make you a puppet, controlled by circumstances, people, and expectations. God wants to restore your individuality, so that you can be free—free to act on principle, free to live a controlled life under Him,

---

1. See John 8:34–36.
2. See Psalm 32:8.

free to pour your energies, talents, and time into the vital priorities of life[3] instead of spending them fruitlessly on the treadmill that society seems to dictate, free to be a partner with Him.[4]

So, in practical terms, how do we enter into that kind of freedom? How do you get from where I was at the beginning of this chapter to the freedom I described in the last paragraph? Let me share with you a simple flowchart that illustrates the process God often takes me through. I'll give it to you piece by piece, and it will all come together by the end of the chapter.

Life today is often like a swirling tornado of duties, expectations, priorities, desires, projects, distractions, entertainment, social relations, and demands. E-mail, pagers, and cell phones crowd work and social obligations into our every waking moment—and even into our sleep time too! Our archenemy, the devil, wants to keep us running at a treadmill pace, never pausing to quietly reflect or to appreciate beauty. He wants us to have no time to think because as long as we have no time to think, we'll keep running through our empty mazes and never get around to the real purpose for our existence. That's why the lists of things to do keep funneling into our schedules until we feel like puppets spinning in a cyclone of activity.

In view of it all, one begins to wonder if it is possible to live a focused life without apology. How do we sort through all this stuff? How do we decide what to do and not do? How do we make a life of real peace and true joy out of so much chaos?

How? It begins by defining your life's purpose!

Life's purpose defined
Gives you deciding power

---

3. See Philippians 3:13, 14.
4. See 1 Corinthians 3:9.

If you are to get a hold on your life, you *must* define the purpose for your life. What are your goals? What are your aspirations, your dreams, and your objectives? Why define your life's purpose? Because knowing your purpose in life is what gives you deciding power—the power to filter everything that comes to your plate and either embrace it or dismiss it.

A lot of people live by "default purposes." They just go with the flow, let it happen, or follow the path of least resistance. Default purposes don't require any special effort, but the outcome is that your life ends up determined by the lowest common denominator of your own impulses and the outside pressures that push you this way or that. When you are ruled by default purposes, you will always be a puppet.

Others go for the gusto. They grab all the gold, glory, and girls that they can. Their life purpose is wrapped up in self-fulfillment. That was me at one time. While I was satisfied with my one girl, I threw myself into grabbing all the gold and glory I could get. My purpose in life was to be successful, wealthy, have notoriety, and fine possessions. I wanted to be in the know, to enjoy travel, recreation, and sports.

I wore myself out, fell out of love with my wife, and didn't know my own children. Pursuing the American dream left me empty and unfulfilled. So I started to look deeper into the lives of those who seemed to have made it the way I wanted to make it. And I found broken men and women—men and women such as Elvis Presley, Marilyn Monroe, Michael Jackson, O. J. Simpson, Richard Nixon, and a host of others that supposedly had it all and had nothing—nothing but shattered lives and broken hearts. My heart went out to them.

I studied the lives of those who were most successful in my profession, and I found men divorced, not merely once or twice, but some even three times. I looked at their families and cried. I saw men not only with broken marriages and wayward children, but broken health as well. I asked myself, "Is this where I'll end up?"

Then I looked at some of those in my own church who held prominent offices and were the "movers and shakers." As I looked past their public identity, I soon discovered what appeared to be the same inner emptiness that I had discerned in my own Christian experience.

God had a serious talk with me, and I listened. I came to the same conclusion Solomon did at the end of his life. (Fortunately for me, I was still in my thirties, with time to reclaim my life.) Solomon stated it like this: "Let us hear the conclusion of the whole matter: Fear God, and keep his commandments: for this is the whole duty of man."[5]

---

5. Ecclesiastes 12:13, KJV.

The whole duty of man? Can this be true? Can life's real purpose and fulfill-ment truly be wrapped up in God rather than centered in self? If so, how does that translate into my everyday life?

I reflected that Jesus had said that keeping the commandments means to love God with every fiber of your being and your neighbor as yourself.[6] So I redefined my life's purpose this way:

1. I would seek a *real walk with God* that brought with it a deep sense of abiding inner peace.
2. I would cultivate an *"in love again"* experience with my wife (my near-est neighbor).
3. I would nurture *a connected family* (my next nearest neighbors) that would stay close in a fragmented and shattered world.
4. I would pursue, without apology, a *simple God-honoring life* filled with depth, meaning, and purpose.
5. I did not want to be the Dead Sea that receives, but never gives. I wanted what I found to flow out and *touch others' lives* (my other neighbors).

This now became my new life. While the practical application of these purposes has changed through the years with the ebb and flow of life, these principles and values have remained my North Star, helping me chart a bal-anced course through all the choices of living. If you are to find a balanced and focused life, you, too, must define the purpose for your life and pursue it with all the zest, vigor, and grace God puts within you.

Your purpose may not be expressed like mine. But you need to identify it, write it down, clarify it, and crystallize it for who you are. My personal assistant expresses her life purpose like this:

To possess the very soul of a pure life right at home and then to spread that influence as far as God opens the way by

- engaging daily with God in heartwork, so that I can bring love, light, and joy into my home and work.
- engaging with my husband to build a solid, vibrant marriage.
- nurturing a connected relationship with my son.
- looking well to the ways of my household, so that it is an inviting place of health, comfort, and rest for all who live or visit there.

---

6. See Matthew 22:37–39.

- putting heart and soul into my work and other relationships to support the spread of the practical gospel to other hearts and homes as well as to feed my own growth in Christ.

My general manager, a thirty-something, single woman with a real zest for life, synthesized her life purpose like this:

My personal mission is to live in the center of God's will, moment by moment. From there, I will share what the power of Jesus does in my life and how God wants to set each of us free to walk in the liberty of heaven. I am committed to live life to the fullest for where I am now and to share the blessings I find with those around me through prioritizing:

- a personal, living and vibrant walk with God.
- relationships with depth and closeness.
- my physical health.
- a restful, clean, and pleasant home.
- financial responsibility, security, and the ability to give.
- adventure and outdoor joys such as hiking, backpacking, and skiing.
- ministry that touches the lives of others.

So what are your values? What is your vision? How would you state your life mission or purpose? If you don't have a clear statement of your purpose in life, you will always be a bit foggy on what to embrace and what to dismiss from your life. Take some time with God—some *quiet* time—to evaluate this. Mull it over, pray it over, think it over, and write it down.

Once you have defined your life's purpose, the most important question to ask yourself repeatedly, daily, of everything that comes to your plate, is, *Is this worthy of my time, attention, energy, and talents?* You must ask yourself this question about a thousand things that invite your attention. There will be scores of topics that consume your time and arouse your interest, but that will detour you from your life's true purpose into a dead end. Everything must now become insignificant in comparison with accomplishing your life's purpose or you will be derailed and stalled again and again. The devil is a genius here, and you must learn to pick up *only* the responsibilities that fall within your life's purpose. Thus, the most important question you will ask yourself daily, multiple times a day is, *Is it worthy?*

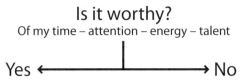

A lot of people get bogged down here. God has a work for them that would bring them genuine fulfillment and joy, but they never get to it because they are unwilling to engage in the necessary discipline. Actually, it's an unwillingness to submit one's life to "the issue" as we discussed in chapter 2. Who's in control? Will circumstances continue to control me, or will I, under God, take control of my life, time, energy, and talents?

Masses of people pass through this life as if they had no definite object to live for, no goals to reach. But you won't climb a mountain until you set your eyes on the summit—and then climb to the top, step by determined step. And you will not reach your life's fulfillment until you set it in concrete—and then let nothing hinder you, stall you, or set you back from gaining it.

Thomas Kinkade, known as the "Painter of Light," is America's most collected living artist. He jealousy guards his time. In his book *Simpler Times,* he mingles his thoughts about life with some of his favorite paintings. He writes, "We were made for calm, not chaos, and that is why we long for simpler times. . . . That's the kind of life I strive to evoke in my paintings. It's the kind of life I'm committed to building for myself and my family."[7]

That's why, he continues, he has learned how to say No. "No, I can't have visitors today. No, I can't attend that meeting. I spend my evenings with my family. No, I can't grant that interview. I need to paint today."[8]

Kinkade has defined his life's purpose, and that gives him his deciding power to ask, Is it worthy? He has developed the ability and muscle to say Yes and No according to his life's purpose and not allow the outside world to dictate his life. This is the next most critical step to a balanced life—the ability to say Yes and No at the right times.

We must all develop the ability to say No to the things that drain our life's purpose and Yes to the things that build it. Many have a hard time saying No when they should, while others can't bring themselves to say Yes even when an opportunity is presented that would take them ten steps forward in their life's purpose. We can be out of balance either way. Fortunately, we are not alone in this struggle. God promises, "I will be with your mouth and teach you

---

7. Anne Christian Buchanan and Thomas Kinkade, *Simpler Times* (Eugene, Ore.: Harvest House Publishers, 1996), 5.

8. Ibid., 14.

what you shall say."[9] Let Him into your thinking as you inquire, Is this worthy of my time, attention, energy, and talents?

Saying No gracefully

This word *No* seems foreign to most of us. In fact, many of us would do well to practice saying it at the beginning of each day. Go ahead, step out on your back porch, and try it. Let's see what it might sound like.

- "No, I can't help with this project. I've promised my wife I'd spend more time with her."
- "No, I can't accept this position, my children need what little time I have after work."
- "No, that new job will require me to travel, and I'll never maintain my health."
- "No, my schedule is full, and there is just no room."
- "No, my spiritual life needs more focus, and this will steal my time with my Lord."
- "No, I really don't need a new car. The old one will suffice."
- "No, a building project would consume me."

What do you need to add to this list? The ability to say No gracefully is absolutely essential to saying Yes to your life's true purpose.

Why is it so hard to say No? Because everyone apparently thinks their hectic pace is a temporary problem, and they are right. It is one temporary problem after another temporary problem after another . . . You know how it goes!

"Jim just started this new business, you know, so it'll take a year to get it going." Temporary problem!

"Well, Susie is in school for two more years, so I've been trying to work to help out with the finances." Temporary problem!

"After I get this next project completed then . . ." Temporary problem!

"We have a new baby in our house, and you know what that means." "When summer is over, there will be more time." "We just bought a new house that we're fixing up ourselves." "We just bought

---

9. Exodus 4:12.

some new land and have to put a home on it." "After this Revelation seminar, cooking class, holiday season . . ." The list goes on and on. The greatest deception we tell ourselves is, *Next week I'll have more time. I just know I will!*

We all think there is a slower day coming as soon as the present obligations are met. But it is an illusion, a mirage we chase! Time proves that the rush is never over—until your health breaks, and you find yourself flat in a bed or laid out in a coffin with no time or ability left to pursue your real purpose.

Really, these temporary problems are often smokescreens for deeper issues. The bottom line is that we are afraid. We are afraid of being misunderstood, of stirring up conflict, of losing out on something, and perhaps, most of all, we are afraid of silence. We know that when we shut down Facebook, the Internet, the TV, overwork, and overcommitment, we are going to have to look ourselves, our spouse, and perhaps our children in the eye. We're going to have to deal with some stuff we don't have a clue how to deal with, and it scares us to death. Will we face our fears with God? Or will we continue to live life our way?

The inability to say No to the outside world ensures that we will say No to God, our spouse, our family, or whatever is our life's purpose.

Delete it

In a letter Martin Luther wrote to his cohort, Melancthon, he declared, "I hate with exceeding hatred those extreme cares which consume you. If the cause is unjust, abandon it!"[10]

If the cause is unjust, delete it. The most used key on my computer keyboard is the delete key. I delete all that is unworthy of my attention, time, energy, and talents.

Is this easy? No. Is it necessary to a focused life? Absolutely! Do some misunderstand? Definitely! But I don't have gospel-hardened children or grandchildren. There is a price to pay for a focused life. Are you willing to pay it? There is also a reward. Are you willing to pursue it? Kay discovered this reality on Facebook. Here's the letter she sent me.

No to Facebook

Dear Jim,

I had been asked so many times at work about why am I not on Facebook. So I signed up the end of last year. Of course, I enjoyed the benefits of contacting friends that I hadn't seen in a long time,

---

10. J. H. Merle d'Aubigne, *History of the Reformation of the Sixteenth Century,* trans. H. White, book 14, chapter 6.

seeing their pictures, etc. My first impression was, "This is so *great!*"

But as I was drawn into it and spent more and more time, I didn't realize what a mistake it was. From the very beginning, God was calling me to not do this, but I resisted. I saw the pop-up ads, which were not at all something I endorsed, but I continued to use Facebook. Then people started sending me things as gifts that were not things I would partake of either, but I persisted. God kept calling me to come to Him and spend time with Him, but I resisted His call. I would get on the computer just to see what people were up to. I even had the application on my iPhone! It was like a drug. Time would get away from me, and I would find myself spending an hour or even two before I realized it.

But my loving God was persistent and kept asking me to spend time with Him instead of this foolishness. I finally listened to God and said, "If You really want me to stop this, show me." I wasn't actually asking God for a sign, but I needed confirmation.

This past May, our family went to hear you talk in Berrien Springs, Michigan, on Mother's Day weekend. Of course, I have heard you talk many times before, but I had never heard you mention anything about Facebook or MySpace. At this particular meeting, if you mentioned Facebook once, you must have mentioned it ten times! I went back to my hotel room that night, and while my family slept, I talked with God. I said, "God, I hear You loud and clear! I want to spend more time with You and my family. Enough of this foolishness!"

The next morning, I deleted the application from my iPhone. When I returned home, I deactivated my account. I was free! Free to spend more time with God, my husband, and my family. My priorities were in the right order again. Several friends asked why I had quit Facebook, and I told them my God and my family are my focus and that Facebook has no place in my life anymore. What a wonderful patient God we serve!

Free at last!
Kay

Dismiss it

No, I'm not "in the know" or on the go like most people are today. In fact, I dismiss more invitations to speak than I accept. Why? Because the "work" or the "cause" or the "group" or the "in crowd" can and will keep me from being *in* Christ and *in love* with my wife and *in control* of my life.

Liquidate it

Why live a simple life? Why liquidate all that excess square footage, tin toys, and trinkets? Simple. Because managing "stuff" controls our life and consumes our time. No, we are not made righteous by a simple life, but simplicity is a tool to redeem time for a righteous life.[11] Jesus lived a very simple life, and we ought to follow Him. He's our supreme Example.

I have a friend who owns six cars—one vehicle for each type of possible use. Yet he can find little time to develop an irresistible marriage. I own one car and have found time to fall in love again with my first love.

Discover what God would have you liquidate in order to fulfill your life's purpose. Then do it.

Suspend it

Some activities may be perfectly moral and proper and even in line with your stated life's purpose. But if they squeeze out your highest priorities, you need to suspend them. Once your main concerns are in order, you can consider adding the extras.

I met a highly successful advertising executive I'll call Margaret. She was vacationing near our home some years ago. As we talked, she was fascinated with our story and what we were discovering in our experiment with God. She went home with a few sermon tapes, and a few days later, our family got a letter from her.

> Dear Jim, Sally, Matthew, and Andrew,
>
> Whether you know it or not, you've been with me all day— through your voice on tape, Jim, and the rest of you in spirit. I've been listening to "Slow Down, Christian" as I *rushed* from a script review meeting to a photo shoot! I had actually scheduled an "after-the-kids-come-home appointment" today. Your lovely sermon spoke so loudly to me that, not only did I cancel the meeting, but I used the time to share your lesson with my boys. And guess what? The client is perfectly happy to meet tomorrow. And the boys are perfectly happy to meet today! Isn't God good!
>
> Margaret

---

11. See Ephesians 5:16, 17.

Yes—prioritize it

Defining your life's purpose and then asking the question *Is it worthy?* will eliminate most of the nonessential stuff that funnels into your life. But I find that there is more that I can say Yes to than I have time or energy to fit into my life. If I try to do everything that fits in my statement of life's purpose, I can still end up too busy and fragmented.

So you must prioritize even those things to which you can answer Yes. My life purpose statement not only spells out my purpose, it also orders my priorities. I have discovered that the ability to prioritize is absolutely essential to experiencing a focused life.

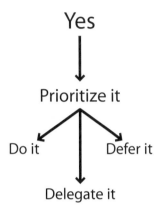

My number one priority is my walk with God. I schedule time every morning to converse with Him and then make it my highest priority throughout the day to maintain sensitivity to His voice. I also set aside a few days at least once a year to go to a remote, high mountain lake to be alone with Him. I call it my "Enoch time." Alone with God, surrounded by His handiwork, I find nothing to distract me. No friends, no family, no phone, no e-mail, no news, not even the daily round of household chores. It's just me and God. My heart breathes, "Speak [Lord]; for thy servant heareth."[12] My regard for this first priority is the source of my direction and empowerment for all the other priorities of my life.

My second priority is Sally. I schedule time daily to find out what's happening in her heart and to nurture a spark of irresistibility between us.

My boys and their families come next. While the boys were at home, we had family time every night at six-thirty. Nothing was allowed to crowd out that time for talking, playing, and connecting with each other. Now that they are grown with homes of their own, I keep my schedule open and flexible to talk with them on the phone and to get together for special events, weekends, or simply a meal.

A simple life without too much stuff supports my other priorities.

The outflow of those first priorities is a ministry that touches others' lives and helps them find the abundant life that Jesus promises.[13]

As you sort through your priorities, write them down. Ingrain them on your frontal lobe. Memorize them. Repeat them to yourself and defend them

---

12. 1 Samuel 3:10, KJV.
13. See John 10:10.

at all costs. Yes, there is a cost to a balanced life.

Jesus told two parables that illustrated this. Both the merchant who found the "pearl of great price" and the laborer who discovered treasure hidden in a field went home and sold everything in order to possess them.[14] There is a big difference between finding something and possessing it. Now you are finding out about a focused life. Are you willing to "sell all" to possess it?

Do it! Take action with the positive

I had to liquidate a lucrative business, a beautiful home on forty parklike acres, five vehicles, and lots of stuff. I had to move to the smallest home I'd ever lived in and survive on the smallest income I'd ever lived on. But guess what? I found myself with lots of time on my hands to devote to my life's purpose.

By God's daily grace and guidance, I applied myself to it. Day in and day out! Fruit started to develop. I stayed on track—not without a lot of attacks, discouragement, distractions, and some derailment. But I always got back on track, and it's working! Praise God, it's working! And it can work for you if you do it! If you do it with all your heart, mind, and soul, you will find it.[15] Then never ever let it go!

Delegate it

My life is a simple life, but it wouldn't be if I didn't delegate. There is so much good, better, and best that crosses my path that I have to either say No or I have to say, "Delegate." God has blessed me with a ministry team that enables me to live out the depth of my commitment while propagating it to others.

To delegate you have to be able to let go and not micromanage the person to whom you have delegated the task. That's not easy for some people. Ask God to show you how and to whom you are to delegate.

Defer it

There are some things that are just too good to say No to and that are too close to your heart to delegate—and yet you don't have enough time to do them. So I have a small list of items I've had to defer until I've freed up some time and energy for them.

Interview with God

Now go—go to Jesus just like Nicodemus did and lay your life, your questions, and your soul out before Him. Have your interview with God. Let Him tell you what He'd have you do to achieve a focused life and find joy in your journey!

---

14. Matthew 13:44–46.
15. See Jeremiah 29:13.

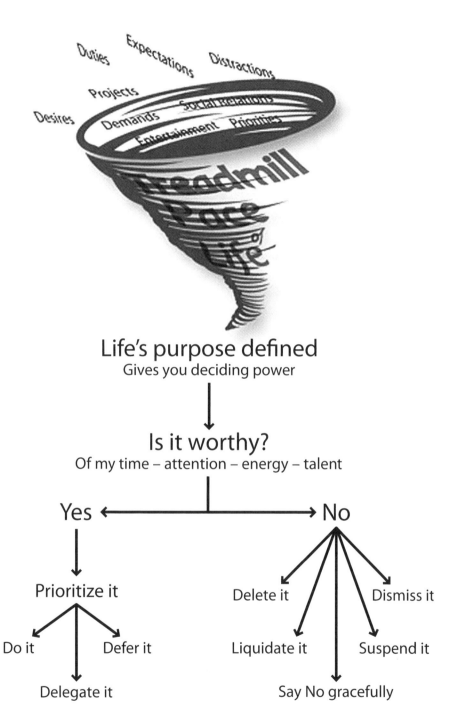

Duties
Expectations
Distractions
Projects
Social Relations
Desires
Demands
Entertainment
Priorities

Treadmill
Race
of
Life

Life's purpose defined
Gives you deciding power

Is it worthy?
Of my time – attention – energy – talent

Yes ← → No

Prioritize it

Do it   Defer it

Delegate it

Delete it   Dismiss it

Liquidate it   Suspend it

Say No gracefully

Questions to ponder or discuss with others:

1. Is your life in balance?
2. Is your life made up of things and getting things done?
3. Are you wearing yourself out on the periphery of life?
4. Do you feel like you're in the swirl of a tornado of duties, demands, expectations, desires, distractions, social relations, projects, priorities, entertainment, and so forth?
5. Do you regularly have time for quiet or reflection, for a pause or for beauty—time to think?
6. Are you prepared to define life's purpose for who you are and where you are right now?
7. Do you believe that deciding on your present life's purpose will give you "deciding power"?
8. Is the question, *Is it worthy of my time, attention, energy, and talents?* something you are prepared to start asking yourself on a regular basis?
9. Do you have the ability to say Yes and No at the right times?
10. Are you willing to begin to delete it, dismiss it, liquidate it, suspend it, or say No gracefully?
11. Will you honestly prioritize your daily life?

Chapter 8

Joy in Your Journey

Now may the God of hope fill you with all joy and peace in believing, that you may abound in hope by the power of the Holy Spirit.

—Romans 15:13

She was thirty years old—attractive, talented, and gifted. She was, perhaps, the most qualified, capable, eligible, unmarried young lady I'd ever met. Her life's dream was to marry a spiritual man—a leader, one who was physically fit and active as well as a good provider—then nurture a family that would honor God. But her dream was unfulfilled with no promise of satisfaction for the foreseeable future.

She was to be the next speaker at the weekend seminar Sally and I were attending. The words *content* and *fulfilled* jumped out at me from the title of her message. I thought to myself, *I've got to hear this! How can this attractive, blond-haired, blue-eyed woman be content and fulfilled when her life's dream has not materialized?*

I listened with an intense interest to enter into her secret.

Are we there yet?

"When I was a little girl, my parents loved to take my sister and me traveling. From our Maryland home we explored the eastern seaboard:

snorkeling in Florida, visiting quaint historical villages in Massachusetts, breathing in the ocean air along Nova Scotia's beautiful beaches, and hiking and camping in Virginia's charming Blue Ridge Mountains. Occasionally our trips took us elsewhere: to California for my aunt's wedding and to Michigan for family reunions. We toured museums in Illinois and gazed in awe at the grandeur of the Canadian Rockies.

"Often as we were driving along, my sister or I would ask, 'Daddy, are we there yet?' We grew weary of the journey, restless in our seats, and we longed to reach our destination—to arrive! So we'd repeat like a broken record, 'Are we there yet?'

"In our restless anticipation, we often missed the simple delights of the journey: deer grazing in a dew-dropped meadow; forests painted in warm autumn hues; the lights of a big city setting the night sky ablaze; the snowy peaks of Colorado towering over our heads; sunshine glistening on a calm lake; birds of all sizes and shapes to identify; or—my dad's favorite suggestions—playing simple games or listening to my mom read a story or my dad talk about his boyhood. Instead of focusing on *getting there,* we could have enjoyed our journey.

"As I've grown older, I've seen my childhood experience played out in life. People say, 'I can't wait for summer. *Then we can . . .*' Or 'when summer is finally over, *we can . . .*' Children say, 'I can't wait to grow up! *Then I will . . .*' How many of you thought, *When I get through college, get married, have a baby, get the children through school, reach retirement,* then I can . . . We focus—not on the present—but on getting through the present to the place where we think we can live happily ever after!

"But there is no such place in this life. Both the past and the future are beyond our reach. We have *this moment*—the only moment we can hold—before it slips through our fingers like sand. If we treasure it, make the most of it, and relish the blessings it brings, we will find a rich life.

"So, instead of restlessly wondering, *Are we there yet?* live life as you go along! Smell more flowers. Kiss your spouse. Hike more mountain trails. Invite a friend over to sip lemonade. Take a refreshing swim in a lake. Write a letter of appreciation to someone you love. Ride your bike into the sunset. Light a candle for your dinner table. Smile at a child. Watch the moon rise in the sky. Laugh more, and put worry away from you. Run down the beach in your bare feet. Embrace each moment as a gift from God." [1]

Empty pursuits

As this woman spoke, I caught on to her secret: find joy in your journey

---

1. Used by permission of Janell Garey.

rather than expecting to find it when you arrive at your final destination.

Powerful! Right on! Out of the ordinary! Everyone needs this! I thought. Why didn't someone explain this to me in my early years? Life could have been so much more meaningful throughout my journey. Instead, I fell right into the trap, the devil's insidious snare, which most people fall for. Future want is the pursuit of mankind.[2]

As I listened to her, a parade of images passed before my mind's eye. Images of all my empty pursuits for fulfillment. The pattern was clear. I would set my sights on some thing or some goal, and I would work to reach that goal or get that thing, sure that when I got it, I would be satisfied, fulfilled, and complete. But that sense of satisfaction was always like a mirage. Just when I thought I was grabbing it, it would vaporize in my hands and pop up somewhere else. I'd go after it again, only to be disappointed once more. It was always just beyond my reach.

The best I can remember, it started at the age of twelve with a brand-new, red and chrome, three-speed Schwinn bicycle. It was the finest bike made in those days. I just knew it would fulfill my every dream! At the age of sixteen, it was a red convertible Pontiac GTO. By the age of eighteen, I had my own cute, playful girlfriend. I was enthralled with her. Surely that would be joy everlasting! On top of that, I was headed for college. With a superior education under my belt, I knew I'd be looked up to, land a high position, and earn a good salary. I thought, *When I get there, I will have arrived!*

But all that time going to school made life a bit tedious, so by the age of twenty-two, I threw myself into adventure sports: scuba diving, downhill skiing, canoeing, camping, hunting, fishing, and exploring the wilderness. Surely all these exciting activities would add the needed spark!

By the time I turned twenty-six, I owned my own business. I loved it! I could call the shots. I had unlimited income potential and freedom; I was highly respected. Surely now my joy would be complete, but something was still lacking.

At the age of twenty-eight, I thought my joy was finally materializing. Sally and I bought a spacious, all-cedar home with cathedral ceilings, a sunken living room, and a grand fireplace. The home was located in the country on forty wooded acres, complete with a pond and orchard.

Looking back now, it's easy to see that I was always chasing after that which was unrealized in my life, believing that my joy would be full when I got to the next destination. Solomon says it well, "Better is an handful with quietness,

---

2. Author's paraphrase of Ellen G. White, *Patriarchs and Prophets* (Mountain View, Calif.: Pacific Press® Publishing Association, 1958), 294.

than both the hands full with travail and vexation of spirit."[3]

As I sat there in that meeting, reviewing the first thirty years of my life, I remembered how life had become overwhelming to me. How it dominated me! How I had experienced much more travail and toil along the way than joy.

Vexation of spirit? Yes, my life along this journey was full of trouble and disquiet with much irritation. Joy? Perhaps a little. But my joy in the present was always pushed to the side by the belief that the next unrealized dream would bring it into full fruition. She was hitting the nail right on my head. Ouch! How about you? Why couldn't I have heard that message when I was thirty? No, better yet, when I was twenty-one? No, when I was twelve? Why didn't anyone tell me? Why are there so few who really understand? Why hadn't my Catholic priest helped me see this? He only sold me on his joy: his church and form of religion. Why hadn't my Protestant pastors brought this to me? They only sold me on their joy: their doctrines, lifestyles, outreach, and church affiliation. Why do so many of us discover true joy so late in our journey? And why do some of us never grasp it at all?

Looking around

As I listened to this young lady speak from her heart and life experience, I looked around at the audience. A lovely young couple about her age caught my attention. Their courtship and wedding had been like a storybook tale. Now they owned a beautiful home in a quiet country setting, had a darling little girl, and excelled in respectable occupations.

But yet, they had little of this joy that was being spoken about. How did I know? They had confided in me. Marriage and family life hadn't fulfilled their dreams. Both of them were pressing toward some unmet goals in their lives. He wanted his own business. She wanted an upscale home.

I thought to myself, *They have everything the young lady in the pulpit desires— marriage, family, a cute nest in the country, each other. Yet they have less truly lasting joy in their daily lives than does the speaker. They're always chasing something and are never satisfied. How can this be? Can't they see what they are missing?*

Nathaniel Hawthorne put it this way: "Happiness is as a butterfly, which when pursued, is always beyond our grasp, but which, if you will sit down quietly, may alight upon you."

What butterfly are you chasing? What do you think you must have before you can be satisfied? Are you so eager for what is to come next that you lose the sweet blessings that are yours now? I'm not speaking against setting goals or

---

3. Ecclesiastes 4:6, KJV.

owning your desires for the future or even working toward fulfilling those desires. But the point is that when we make our *joy* contingent on *tomorrow,* we risk getting to the end of our lives never having fully grasped what we sought, because tomorrow is always just beyond our fingertips.

Looking around again

I looked behind me, and my eyes fell on a couple in their late fifties. By worldly standards, they were very successful. They were worth millions, owned a lovely home on a beautiful lake, and were highly respected in the business community.

Yet they had come to me for counsel because their lives were troubled with much travail and vexation. Their children had both left the church. Their marriage was a mess, and she wanted a divorce.

If you could have rewound the clock to their courtship, you would have seen that they both were chasing the butterfly of marriage. But once they got it, they turned their sights on the next butterfly that was just beyond their grasp and never fully entered into the gift that was their present. Instead of *living out* their joy, they *crowded it out* by pursuing the next butterfly.

Are we displacing what we have with the desire for that which we have not? Have we bought into the devil's myth: "In the day ye eat thereof, then your eyes shall be opened, and ye shall be as gods"?[4]

The devil is quite a salesman. He's a liar too. A subtle liar! In their perfect state, Adam and Eve bought into his sophistry. They had perfect health, a perfect spouse, a perfect environment, a perfect occupation, and a perfect connection with God. Yet they bought into the devil's lie! *"When . . . then . . ."* And all of us have inherited our first parents' weakness.

What is the Holy Spirit saying to you right now? Have you been bypassing the joy in your journey? I had. This young couple was. This older couple was paying the price. But all of us can still find it, if we choose to. It's never too late to open our present and enter into its joy!

Pulpit talk

You may be wondering, *Is this just pulpit talk? It sounds good in theory, but does it deliver in real life?*

I can honestly tell you, "Yes, it delivers!"

This young lady is Janell Garey, our ministry's general manager.[5] We've

---

4. Genesis 3:5, KJV.

5. Her recorded live message is on the album *Choosing Your Destiny,* which you can order from Empowered Living Ministries.

known her since she was thirteen years old. Does she have real longings and desires? Yes! Does she want to find that special man, marry, have children, and raise a family to God's glory? Yes! In fact, she actively invests herself in those dreams. Her desires, goals, and aspirations are healthy and God given. So are many of yours.

However, if the pursuit of future wants leads us to discount our present joy and happiness, we are deceived. Genuine joy and fulfillment have but one source—God. When you have Him, you have everything![6] We can be content with what we have at the present.

"One's life does not consist in the abundance of the things he possesses."[7] It consists of Christ![8] "A little that a righteous man has is better than the riches of many wicked."[9] That's why the Scriptures clearly state, "Now may the God of hope fill you with all joy and peace in believing, that you may abound in hope by the power of the Holy Spirit."[10]

It is the Holy Spirit that imparts joy and peace—not circumstances, things, or accomplishments. That's why God declares, "Now may . . . you" have—not partial joy and peace, not 85 percent joy and peace—but "*all* joy and peace in believing." Believing what? That God is real, that He is good, and that He is in touch with your life. Embracing that belief, I can embrace each day as it unfolds from His hand. Both the things that bring us godly pleasure and the disappointments that we feel to the depths of our soul are gifts from His hand intended for good. We may open each new day as His present to us and find joy in it. That's *the naked gospel*!

It is from Jesus that I receive life. It is in Him that I live and move and have my being.[11] Whether or not I get my front-loading washer and dryer, I can have joy. Now! Today! This moment!

Don't be deceived. If I stake my joy on getting my washer and dryer, I have substituted the gift for the Giver. I have said by my actions and/or attitude that I know what I need better than God does and that He is not sufficient for me. Many, if not most, live by this premise. God is not enough for them. They turn His gifts into idols and endlessly chase their substitutionary joys: a perfect spouse, children, a home free of debt, a home in the country, a position of influence and power, sex, wealth, prominence, being someone, a new wardrobe, solving

---

6. See Colossians 2:10.
7. Luke 12:15.
8. See Colossians 3:4.
9. Psalm 37:16.
10. Romans 15:13.
11. See Acts 17:28.

their health problems, or even overcoming their character defects so that they feel like the perfect Christian.

The essence of the naked gospel is that possessions, positions, people, places, performance, and pleasure cannot fill us. God is the only One who can fill us! My joy is full when my soul is at rest with God and my flesh is subdued in Christ!

Can Janell be complete now, presently, in her current circumstances? Yes! Are her longings and desires wrong? Only if they control and override the joy of the Lord in the present!

Finding joy

Back to that meeting. Janell went on to share how she found joy in her journey by choosing to shift her thinking from self-condemning and disappointed thoughts to focusing on singleness as an opportunity. She recognized that God has given her an extended time to work for Him as a single woman.

She has watched her friends court, marry, and start families. She has relished the precious opportunities that having her own home and family would offer. But rather than nurture her disappointment over being denied this privilege, she turned to God and prayed, "Lord, let me do all You intend me to accomplish in my extended time of singleness. I do not know what is in Your plan for me, but I want to do it with all my heart, strength, and will. If it is in Your plan for me to be married, I want to stand at the altar and be able to say, 'In the time of singleness You've given me, I have done what I know You wanted me to accomplish.' "

As she expressed this surrender to God's will, her attitude toward her present state changed. She began to view her journey as an opportunity to make the most of the time given to her as a single person. Regardless of her status or circumstances, her purpose in life became to follow God's revealed will for her life and find joy in her journey.

As she did this, her attitude toward her current state changed. She *did* find joy! She tells me that she can honestly say that her life is not boring, unfulfilling, discontented, or empty even though she is not yet at the "destination." As she opens her "present," she has found real fulfillment and joy—where she is right now!

She relishes the blessings of today: a gentle sunrise, a smile from her co-worker, an e-mail interaction with someone who is struggling and whom she can point to Jesus, a bird coming to her feeder, the good health God has given her, the delicate snowflakes lacing a tree branch, an encouraging phone call, a fresh flower along her foot path, the opportunity to train a child how to finish his plate of food cheerfully, a sweet note from a friend, a job that challenges and fulfills her, and trials that help her to grow.

These are some of the ways she has turned what could be a very discouraging and lonely time in her life into a time of service and fulfillment. She is content, fulfilled, and finding joy in her journey as a single woman!

The blank

Actually, the full title for Janell's sermon was "Content, Fulfilled, and _____." At first she had titled it, "Content, Fulfilled, and Single." But then she realized that not everyone in her audience was single and wanting to be married, but that everyone has something they could put in that blank.

What would you put in the blank? Content, Fulfilled, and Childless? Homeless? Sick? Friendless? Poor? Unemployed? Bored? Mortgaged? Out of Shape? Brokenhearted? Maybe your title would be "Content, Fulfilled, While a Nobody." Whatever your present condition that you wish were different, put it in that blank and then surrender it to God. Find out through the naked gospel how you can be content and fulfilled even while that longing—legitimate as it is—is denied.

Janell fills in her blank, not with some future goal, some butterfly she wants, but with the joy of the present that she is experiencing now. This is her present! She opens this present, this gift that God has given her, and enjoys it to the fullest as she lives out day by day the experience into which He guides her. You, too, can find joy, rest, peace, and quietness in your present condition, knowing that "God shall supply all your need."[12]

Embracing your "blank"

The apostle Paul learned this secret. He said, "I have learned in whatever state I am, to be content: I know how to be abased, and I know how to abound. Everywhere and in all things I have learned both to be full and to be hungry, both to abound and to suffer need. I can do all things through Christ who strengthens me."[13]

Paul did not say this lightly. He faced some real adversities as a frontline missionary. He reports,

> From the Jews five times I received forty stripes minus one. Three times I was beaten with rods; once I was stoned; three times I was shipwrecked; a night and a day I have been in the deep; in journeys

---

12. Philippians 4:19.
13. Philippians 4:11–13.

often, in perils of waters, in perils of robbers, in perils of my own countrymen, in perils of the Gentiles, in perils in the city, in perils in the
wilderness, in perils in the sea, in perils among false brethren; in weari-
ness and toil, in sleeplessness often, in hunger and thirst, in fastings
often, in cold and nakedness—besides the other things, what comes
upon me daily: my deep concern for all the churches.[14]

How would you like to have some of those things in your blank? These are
not exactly what we might consider good fringe benefits! I wouldn't blame
Paul if he had longed once in a while for a quiet, peaceful retirement. But that
was not Paul's attitude.

Paul embraced his "blank," declaring, "Most gladly I will rather boast in my
infirmities, that the power of Christ may rest upon me. Therefore I take pleasure in infirmities, in reproaches, in needs, in persecutions, in distresses, for
Christ's sake. For when I am weak, then am I strong."[15] Paul knew, without a
shadow of a doubt, where his fulfillment came from.

You see, Paul had caught a lot of the butterflies that most Jews in his day
pursued—and he knew how empty they were. He was "circumcised the eighth
day, of the stock of Israel, of the tribe of Benjamin, a Hebrew of the Hebrews;
concerning the law, a Pharisee; concerning zeal, persecuting the church; concerning the righteousness which is in the law, blameless."[16]

But when Paul discovered *the naked gospel,* he saw the worthlessness of substituting the gifts for the Giver. He continued, "I count all things . . . but dung,
that I may win Christ, and be found in him, not having mine own righteousness, which is of the law, but that which is through the faith of Christ, the
righteousness which is of God by faith: That I may know him, and the power
of his resurrection, and the fellowship of his sufferings."[17]

Present joy

You and I need to find what Paul found. Yes, he had a high calling. Yes, he
had a glorious purpose to his life. But he would have lost sight of his calling and
never experienced that purpose if he had insisted on finding contentment and
fulfillment in some future destination free from disappointment, hardship, un-
fairness, and circumstances that would drown most people in despair!

---

14. 2 Corinthians 11:24–28.
15. 2 Corinthians 12:9, 10.
16. Philippians 3:5, 6.
17. Philippians 3:8–10, KJV.

Paul had learned that his sufficiency was in God.[18] And that God was able to meet all his need![19] This was the secret of his contentment.

Wow! I'm impressed. I want some of his blood! That's the blood of Jesus not only covering him, but also flowing through him. That's the *naked gospel* applied in daily living. It means you can be content and fulfilled in whatever your blank may be.

Like Janell and Paul, our desires need not displace our present joy in the Lord. We may trust that God is sufficient to fulfill all our needs and desires in His timing and by His grace! That's a living faith—a faith that controls the thoughts and emotions and does not allow future wants to banish present joys. That's power! That's the power of God in and through you!

But why does God not give us what we want—especially when our desires are legitimate? I believe that when our blank is not being filled, it can have the effect of weaning us from this world. It heightens our hunger for God. That longing, restless feeling that we attach to our butterflies is really a longing for God. Those butterflies can be the idols or substitutes that stand between God and us. When we can be content with our "blank," then God can truly fill us with His joy and possibly grant our desires.

Isn't that why God asked Abraham to sacrifice Isaac—the fulfillment of his fondest hopes and dreams? No, God didn't want Isaac. God wanted Abraham! And God wants you—all of you. And sometimes He seems to withdraw Himself from you in order to activate you!

---

18. See 2 Corinthians 3:5; 9:8.
19. See Philippians 4:19.

Questions to ponder or discuss with others:

1. Can you be content and fulfilled when your life's dream has not materialized?
2. Can you find joy in your journey and not just at your hoped-for destination?
3. Are future wants your pursuit and focus?
4. Have you found the quest to fulfill your pursuits leaving you empty—even after they are fulfilled?
5. Why do so many of us discover only late in our journey what true joy really is?
6. How many people do you know who presently possess true joy?
7. What "butterflies" are you chasing?
8. Has the joy of your wedding day vanished? Why?
9. Have you been missing the joy in your journey?
10. Is it the Holy Spirit who imparts joy and peace, or do those things come from circumstances, things, and accomplishments?
11. Like Solomon, do you really believe that apart from experiencing oneness with God, "all is vanity"?

Chapter 9

When God Seems Silent

My God, My God, why have You forsaken Me?
Why are You so far from helping Me,
And from the words of My groaning?
O My God, I cry in the daytime, but You do not hear;
And in the night season, and am not silent.

—Psalm 22:1, 2

hat is it about a life of faith that keeps demanding more of us—greater testing, deeper searching, and more dependence? Why is it that God can be so real, so personal, and so present with us at times, and at other times, seem so distant and silent?

When God leads us beside still waters and makes us lie down in green pastures, it's easy to trust and follow where He goes.[1] But when He asks us to walk in the darkness,[2] our faith is tested to its utmost. Yet when I look back on my own experience, those dark, silent times have been some of the most effective catalysts for finding the depth with God that I have prayed for.

Different people perceive God's silence differently. I'm a "get things done in the most efficient way possible" kind of guy. For me, God seems nearest when things are happening, when He's giving me

---

1. See Psalm 23:1, 2.
2. Isaiah 50:10.

the solutions I need for the problems I face, when difficult situations are being resolved, when life moves forward positively and efficiently, and when trials are kept to a minimum. I like it when things are happening, and they're happening well!

For others, it's not so much the events taking place in their lives that signal God's silence as it is the absence of an emotional perception of His presence. When they can sense His smile, feel His embrace, and hold His hand, they can face whatever may come. But when that emotional connection is gone, it seems that God has lost interest in them, that He's standing by passively, preoccupied with other business, is angry, or just doesn't really care. That feeling of emotional abandonment can be crushing. Job experienced it and expressed it like this:

"Oh, that I knew where I might find Him,
That I might come to His seat! . . .

"Look, I go forward, but He is not there,
And backward, but I cannot perceive Him;
When He works on the left hand, I cannot behold Him;
When He turns to the right hand, I cannot see Him."[3]

The Scriptures affirm that Job was a perfect and upright man, who feared God and abstained from evil,[4] yet he honestly struggled with God's silence— both from the perspective of unexplained and overwhelming losses and from the sense of disconnection with God.

We often interpret silence according to our experiences with other people. People often get quiet when they are angry, when they disagree with something we have done or said, or when they don't think we're worth talking to. Silence indicates withdrawal, disconnection, even rejection or abandonment. It can mean, "I don't care about you. I won't help you. You're on your own."

Sometimes when we're experiencing the natural consequences of our own sins and poor choices—or those of others—we can feel silence and condemnation from God. Our experience with discipline in the past may have left in us a tendency to perceive God negatively when He allows us to reap what we have sown.

Jeremiah felt that. Even though he was a faithful prophet, he experienced God's judgments upon Judah right along with everybody else. He mourned,

3. Job 23:3, 8, 9.
4. Job 1:1.

I am the man who has seen affliction by the rod of His wrath.
He has led me and made me walk
In darkness and not in light.
Surely He has turned His hand against me
Time and time again throughout the day.[5]

Was God condemning Jeremiah? No! "There is therefore now no condemnation to those who are in Christ Jesus."[6] But Jeremiah *felt* condemnation. He *felt* God's displeasure, and it caused him intense suffering.

Whatever silence means to you, there will be times in your life when God seems silent, and you feel alone. If you feel singled out during those times, don't! The reality is that God is very much with you and is doing a deeper work in you. He hasn't left you. He hasn't forsaken you. The promises in His Word are just as sure when He seems silent as when He seems very much present.

Like Job, we may not always understand what's happening behind the scenes, but we can rely on God's Word anyway. That's how Jesus handled God's apparent silence. When He fasted in the desert for forty days, He relied on the Word of God stored in His mind, and on the affirmation of the Holy Spirit that He had received on the banks of the Jordan following His baptism.

This is what we must do in those silent times too. And when we do, we allow God to work through the agony of trial and delay to activate within us those attributes that are more precious than gold.[7] Let me share with you five things that God's silence can activate in our lives as I've experienced or observed in those deeply searching silent times.

1. Silence activates faith

I think of Abram (later known as Abraham) when God called him to leave all that was familiar to him and move to a country God would show him. What a man of faith! If you had met that seventy-five-year-old man on the streets of Haran, as he headed out with his camel train loaded with all his stuff, and had asked him where he was going, he probably would have said something like, "I'm not sure. I'm simply following God as He leads."[8] We may think Abram was being a bit presumptuous, but in hindsight it's obvious that he was moving by faith—faith in a God that always provides.

---

5. Lamentations 3:1–3.
6. Romans 8:1.
7. See 1 Peter 1:7.
8. See Genesis 12:1.

Then God kept promising Abram that He was going to give all this land to his posterity. One day, Abram reminded God that he had no children. God promised Abram that through his seed would come the Messianic nation and that his descendants would be as numberless as the stars of heaven.[9] Wow! What a promise!

And God not only made the promise, but He changed Abram's name to *Abraham,* which means "father of a multitude." He changed the name of Abraham's wife from *Sarai* to "Sarah," indicating that she would be the mother of kings and nations.[10] By this time, Abraham was ninety-nine years old, and Sarah was eighty-nine.

Can you imagine what it was like for them to be introduced to new friends? "Hi, I'm the 'Father of a multitude' and this is my wife, 'Mother of nations and kings.' "

"Well, it's nice to meet you! How many children do you have?"

"Uh, well . . . none yet."

But in spite of appearances, Abraham believed God. Still, no offspring came. Had God forgotten His promise? Was He really there? Had Abraham heard correctly? Silence.

Some time later, God again promised Abraham and Sarah that the son of promise would come through their seed.[11] Sarah, past child-bearing years, laughed at the thought. *"It's too late!"*[12]

But then, when it was far beyond human possibility for them to conceive a child, God "visited" the old couple, and Isaac, the long-awaited heir was conceived![13] The silence was finally broken!

Why? Why was God so silent? Why the long delay?

Is God silent in your life? He has been in mine.

I remember when Sally and I first caught the glimpse of a simpler life. We knew God was calling us to the wilderness, so we set out to find that special place—our promised land, if you will. After discovering our remote mountain valley, we went back home to sell our house, business, and possessions.

Then silence—nothing! No sale! Not one interested buyer! We had a lovely place in the country: forty wooded, parklike acres with a pond and a spring on a dead-end road; complete with a beautiful log home, garage, and outbuildings; all within twenty minutes of a growing, thriving city center.

---

9. See Genesis 15:5.
10. See Genesis 17:5, 15, 16.
11. See Genesis 18:10.
12. See Genesis 18:12.
13. See Genesis 21:1, 2.

No one was interested. No takers showed up. No offers were made—not even one! Twelve months of dead silence went by. We were confused.

Then, when we had given up hope that our place would sell and had stopped trying, God sent someone to us. Why? Why couldn't God have sent that someone up front?

In retrospect, we can see that the waiting time activated our faith. It deepened our trust. It brought us to an absolute dependence on God to fulfill what He had shown us. He wanted us surrendered to Him! He wanted us to know He was the One in charge! Silence can be a tool in the hand of God to activate and deepen your faith, trust, and dependence.

Abraham and Sarah could take no credit for the son of promise and the Messianic nation. Jim and Sally could take no credit for the blessings that followed as our new life was established. When God tests our faith with silence and delay, we have an opportunity to see whether our trust is true and sincere or if it is changeable like the waves of the sea.

We are to wait for the Lord—not in fretful anxiety, but in quiet, trusting faith. God must be the preeminent One—not us or our talents and abilities![14] The words of the song "Trust His Heart"[15] say it so well:

> God is too wise to be mistaken;
> God is too good to be unkind.
> So when you don't understand,
> When you don't see His plan,
> When you can't trace His hand,
> Trust His heart.

2. Silence activates dross burning

Moses was a man's man with a triple type A personality. He was used to giving orders and getting things done—building sturctures and winning battles and mastering just about any challenge the Egyptian court could muster. The Scriptures say, "And Moses was learned in all the wisdom of the Egyptians, and was mighty in words and in deeds."[16] Moses did not just passively soak up the training he was given. He energetically took hold of the opportunities placed before him and honed his knowledge and skill until he was without peer as a general, a statesman, a poet, and a philosopher.

Yet Moses knew that his destiny was not to be a pharaoh. He knew his

---

14. See Isaiah 2:22.
15. Babbie Mason, "Trust His Heart," *Timeless,* Spring Hill Music Group © 2001.
16. Acts 7:22.

purpose was to deliver a demoralized, ragged bunch of slaves from bondage. His life's calling was treason to Egypt and death to his worldly prospects, but, by faith, he saw that God was a bigger reward than all of Egypt. "Moses, when he became of age, refused to be called the son of Pharaoh's daughter."[17] That was faith! That was courage! That decision revealed Moses as a man with moral fiber and independence. He didn't just follow the crowd. He chose God over the world. What a man!

From a human standpoint, Moses was the ideal deliverer for Israel. He knew it too. And that was the fatal flaw that shunted him into the wilderness of Midian for forty years.[18] The attribute that Moses, and those who looked up to him, valued most was the dross God needed to burn out of him—his self-confidence. Moses believed that he knew how to deliver God's people and that he just needed God to bless his plans. He was in charge. He was "the one." How many of us have the same problem Moses had—we make our plans without consulting God, then we bow our heads and ask God to bless them?

Moses was so sure of himself that God had to put him in a time-out in the wilderness with a bunch of stupid sheep for forty years. Of course, Moses didn't know that his time in the wilderness would last for forty years. As far as he was concerned, his life's mission was lost, and he'd be sitting in the wilderness for the duration of his time on earth. Can you imagine what that must have been like for a man of his character and experience? I think it must have driven him nuts—at least to start with. And God didn't tell him the end of the story. Moses had to deal with the open-ended silence, not knowing God's final purpose for him.

Moses' preeminence was so strong that it took forty years of silence to burn it out of him. But he entered into this new school with the same tenacity that he had approached every other challenge in his life. At first, he didn't understand what he was supposed to be learning, but as the years rolled on, he became small in his own eyes and God became bigger and bigger. Then, when Moses was completely at rest with the prospect of a lifetime of caring for smelly sheep, God called him back to the front lines.

This time, though, Moses was truly ready. Now he was self-distrustful, timid, and slow of speech. He was afraid to bring self into the picture. He had received his "PhD": the "portrait of His Divinity." Now God could use Moses. Now his Egyptian training filled its proper place—under *God's* direction. And God, using Moses, led His people out of Egypt with a mighty hand!

The most difficult dross-burning lessons I have had to learn, once Sally and

---

17. Hebrews 11:24.
18. See Acts 7:29, 30.

I arrived in our "resting place," have not been wilderness living, working through the mazes of religion, or discovering the naked gospel. I can honestly say that, for me, the hardest dross burning has been entering into and living a life in which I see myself as self-distrustful, unworthy, and inefficient.

God uses silence in our lives for dross burning. If you find yourself in this silence, embrace it. Don't shun it. Use it as the tool God intends it to be. Is it comfortable? No! Is it needed? Yes! How many let it have its work? Very few.

The lessons God taught Moses are the lessons He wants to teach you and me. We all must become pliable in God's hands. Many of us are overconfident. We're confident in our church, confident in our understanding, and confident in our abilities. We have more confidence in ourselves than we do in God.

God uses times of silence for us to do soul searching and dross burning, so that our confidence may rest in Him and Him only! We must come to honestly see ourselves as incompetent to run our own lives. "Our sufficiency is from God."[19]

The prayer of our hearts needs to be, "Lord, I can't do anything without You. I dare not even speak without filtering all my words through You. You are the efficient One. Teach me to rely wholly upon you. Teach me to be swift to hear You, slow to speak my own words, and slow to anger[20] that I may honor You in all I say and do. Teach me to be timid, fearful that I might bring self into the work and dishonor Your name. Help me to be cautious of allowing my own preeminence to take over and to be humble of my own estimate of myself. Teach me, Lord, to always live under You, in You, and through You!"

3. Silence activates the conscience

The conscience is our God-given ability to discern between right and wrong; it is intended to be God's voice to our souls. It can lead to feelings of remorse when we do things that go against our moral values, and it can lead to feelings of integrity when we do what we know to be right. A good, pure, and enlightened conscience is a wonderful gift from God to help us make wise decisions that keep us in the path of right.[21]

By itself, however, the conscience is not a safe guide. The conscience can

---

19. 2 Corinthians 3:5.

20. See James 1:19.

21. See 1 Timothy 3:9; Hebrews 9:14.

be seared,[22] defiled,[23] or weakened,[24] so that people can partake of the basest sins without remorse. The conscience is only as reliable as the authority to which it is allied.

Adolf Eichmann, sometimes referred to as "the architect of the Holocaust," was charged by Hitler's administration with the task of facilitating and managing the logistics of mass deportation of Jews to ghettos and extermination camps in German-occupied Eastern Europe. After the war, he fled to Argentina and lived there under a false identity. He was captured by Israeli Mossad operatives in Argentina and tried and convicted in an Israeli court on fifteen criminal charges.

Speaking in his own defense, Eichmann said that he did not dispute the facts of what happened during the Holocaust. During the whole trial, Eichmann insisted that he was only "following orders." He explicitly declared that he had abdicated his conscience in order to follow the *Führerprinzip*—a philosophy of political authority in which one yields unquestioning obedience to his superior.[25]

Adolf Eichmann may be an extreme example, but most people do not realize the extent to which they have aligned their consciences to a relative, a corporation, an employer, a church, or something else besides God and His Word. We do well to examine the authority we have accepted for our conscience.

During cross-examination, Eichmann was asked "if he considered himself guilty of the murder of millions of Jews. He replied: 'Legally not, but in the human sense . . . yes, for I am guilty of having deported them.' " One piece of evidence was a quote in which Eichmann stated, " 'I will leap into my grave laughing because the feeling that I have five million human beings on my conscience is for me a source of extraordinary satisfaction.' "[26] (How sick!)

Hannah Arendt, a reporter for the *New Yorker,* attended Eichmann's trial, and her reporting became the basis of her book *Eichmann in Jerusalem.* A Jew herself, Arendt concluded that Eichmann showed no trace of an anti-Semitic personality or of any psychological damage to his character. At his trial, he appeared to have a common, ordinary personality, displaying neither guilt nor hatred. She suggested that many of the great evils in history, and the Holocaust in particular, were not executed by fanatics or sociopaths, but rather by ordinary people who

---

22. See 1 Timothy 4:2.

23. See Titus 1:15.

24. See 1 Corinthians 8:10, 12.

25. Wikipedia, "Adolf Eichmann," Wikipedia, http://en.wikipedia.org/w/index .php?title=Adolf_Eichmann&oldid=358242777 (accessed April 26, 2010).

26. Ibid.

accepted the premises of their state and therefore participated in these evils with the view that their actions were normal.

Eichmann made the grave error of aligning his conscience with a malignant and evil authority—with the result that he was able, in "good conscience," to take delight in unfathomable atrocities.

Saul made a similar mistake. He aligned his conscience with the authority of bigoted religious leaders and "breathing out threatenings and slaughter against the disciples of the Lord"[27] requested permission to spread his terror to Damascus— thinking he was doing God a service.

But on Saul's way there, God boldly confronted him. In a flash, he saw that his conscience had been allied with a false authority. He spent the next three days in darkness and an agony that made those days seem like years.[28] During those three long days, Saul's conscience was activated and realigned. Again and again, he recalled, with anguish of spirit, the part he had taken in the martyrdom of Stephen. With horror, he thought of his guilt in allowing himself to be controlled by the malice and prejudice of the priest and rulers. He closely examined himself in the light of Scripture and humbled his heart before God.

When those three days ended, Saul was a different man. He had become Paul. The things that had formerly delighted him were now disgusting, and what he had hated, he now embraced. Instead of depending on his own proud pharisaical performance, he relied wholly on God to write His law of love upon his heart. He came forth determined henceforth "to have always a conscience void of offense toward God, and toward man."[29]

When God is silent in my life, the first place I look is to my conscience. *Lord, is there something blocking You from working in my life? Lord, have I tied Your hands? Have I unwittingly allied my conscience to someone or something apart from You and the principles expressed in Your Word? Lord, is it me?*

Times of silence, whether they last forty years or three days, are used by God to help us review our past lives, to see the error of our ways, and to repent. Repentance must have its rightful place in our lives. Repentance begins with aligning our conscience with God and His principles as expressed in the Scriptures. It deepens as we surrender all we know to Him. Nothing withheld! One hundred percent God's! I know many Christians who are 50 percent aligned with God. I know some Christians who are 75 percent His. There are few Christians who are 100 percent His.

---

27. Acts 9:1, KJV.
28. See Acts 9:9.
29. Acts 24:16, KJV.

That's why God bids us to "be still and know" that He is God.[30] We've got to tune into His frequency, so that we can individually hear Him speaking to our hearts. He wants to educate our consciences to be safe and trustworthy—and we need silence for that to happen.

That's why I take my "Enoch time." I backpack to a remote wilderness lake with the bare essentials and God's Word for three or four days. There is nothing to distract me. No phone calls; no e-mail; no friends, family, or ministry; no TV, radio, or DVDs. Just quiet, blessed silence. In that time alone with God, the issues and needs of my life become clearer. My conscience is activated, and its misalignments become apparent. I find direction for areas where I need to clear, enlighten, and realign my conscience.

It's good medicine! Those who have taken my recommendation to do likewise have found answers for their lives—not always the answers they were looking for, but the solutions God wants to deliver.

4. Silence activates patience

Have you ever prayed, "Lord, give me patience—and I want it right now"? We all chuckle at that request because we inherently know that patience is developed only by the exercise of it. That's why James says, "Count it all joy when you fall into various trials, knowing that the testing of your faith produces patience. But let patience have its perfect work, that you may be perfect and complete, lacking nothing."[31]

Often we associate our trials with God's silence. When He's allowing us to be stretched to the point of discomfort, it seems that He is silent. Actually, He is very active in our lives—just not in the way we want or expect to see! When we allow the silence to deepen our trust, burn our dross, and realign our conscience, we are developing a patience that is a positive steadfastness that bravely waits on God. This is letting patience have its perfect work.

Those of us who don't receive an immediate answer to our prayers and become discouraged, need to study the life of Joseph, David, and Job. Talk about activating patience!

Think of Joseph! God gave him a dream that all his brothers would some day bow before him, and then he was sold into slavery by those very brothers. He had entered his school of silence. He determined to deepen his faith in God, to embrace character growth, and to keep his conscience allied with heaven. For years, he was Potiphar's best slave—to the extent that Potiphar put him in charge of his entire household. Potiphar prospered under Joseph's

---

30. Psalm 46:10.
31. James 1:2–4.

management. Things were looking up for this favored son turned slave.

Then, Joseph's fidelity to principle landed him in jail under false accusation. The silence in his life deepened. As far as Joseph knew, he would spend the rest of his life locked up. Any hope for reconnecting with his family or seeing his dreams come true must have vanished. Would you have been tempted to despair? I would. I'm sure Joseph was, too, but he didn't stay there. He refused to sink into a sad and discouraged state of mind. He continued to calmly trust God and to pick up the opportunities for excellence that he found in the dungeon.

After years in prison, Joseph was brought before the king and rewarded with the office of prime minister of Egypt. What a turn of events! Patience in silence had had its perfect work in Joseph. The character formed by his patient endurance through hopeless circumstances could never have been forged in easier times.

God often allows delay for our benefit. Under duress, we can more easily identify the weak links in the chain of our character. We find out whether our patience is true and sincere or as changeable as the waves of the ocean.

These experiences are not merely for the great ones of ancient times. They are for us ordinary folks, for you and me. We must all learn to wait for the Lord, not in fretful anxiety over our present state, but in an undaunted faith that withstands the silence. And as we do, we find that silence activates our freedom.

5. Silence activates freedom

I lay in my bed for two whole days. I didn't get up except to relieve myself. I didn't sleep—even at night. The tears would not stop flowing. Matthew and Angela stood at the foot of my bed. "Father, this is not like you. You need to get up. You need to eat. You need to take care of yourself." They were afraid I was going to die.

I hadn't really slept in months. My whole nervous system was a mess—I was on edge. When you get to that place, you just want the pressure off! I was facing the loss of three things I didn't think I could live without—my reputation, my comfort, and my position in life. My whole being recoiled at the thought. I didn't think I could face it. It would be worse than annihilation; it would be a living hell.

The devil had me between a rock and a hard place, and it seemed that God was silent. The devil was weighing how badly I wanted out of my agony, and it appeared that I had two choices: First, hold on to my integrity and lose everything. Second, sell out my integrity and get momentary relief.

A lot of you face those kinds of choices too. Many take the devil's way out. That's why the use of illicit drugs and alcohol is on the increase. That's why the divorce rate is so high. That's why the entertainment and competitive sports industries prosper. That's why so many people become puppets of others and lose control over their own consciences. People are looking for easy escapes, and the devil is all too willing to provide them.

The redeeming value of agony is that it takes you down to the real bottom-line questions, such as Am I going to live on the naked Word of God, believing that He loves me and that He will bring the needed relief in His own time?

God seemed silent, but He really wasn't. He was just speaking on a frequency I didn't want to tune into right then. He was saying, *"Jim, I'm not at all worried about your reputation, your comfort, or your position in life. Your finances are no big deal. Don't worry about any of that! Don't be anxious. Trust Me. None of those things need to disturb you. Do you want to be free?"*

My frequency went something like this: "It's not right! It's not fair! Everything I've worked so hard for is being taken from me. This can't happen. Why won't God intervene? Not worry? How can a man who is focused, driven, and goal oriented *not* worry when everything is going down the tubes? Let's get real!"

As I agonized further, I began to tune into God. He was saying, *"Jim, do you really believe that I'll fight for you?"*

"It doesn't look like it, Lord. It looks more like You are betraying me."

"Jim, do you want real freedom or do you want security?"

Was oneness with God my primary motivation? God did have a way through the darkness, but I had to trust Him fully, even though it felt like He was slaying me.

Finally, I made my choice. By faith I decided that the naked Word of God held more weight than appearances and circumstances. "Seek the Kingdom of God above all else, and live righteously, and he will give you everything you need."[32]

"OK, Lord. My reputation is not important. Finances are not important. Position is not important. I have You!"

You know what? My agony went away. Nothing about the situation changed. In fact, it got a lot worse before it got better, but I was a free man! It got scary at times. When I was being gouged, it hurt. It took years to work out the losses. But God used that silence to free me.

What is He saying to you in your silence? Are you tuned in to His frequency? What is the devil tempting you to sell out in order to get temporary relief? Don't do it. By holding on to your faith in God, by allowing the fiery trial to burn away your dross, by keeping your conscience aligned with God,

---

32. Matthew 6:33, NLT.

and by not becoming impatient, you will find a greater freedom than you can possibly imagine.

God has a purpose in your silence. He wants to bring you forth as gold purified in the fire—just like He did with Abraham, Moses, Paul, Joseph, and others. When He brought them out of their silence, it wasn't just so they could admire their polished gold! He had a work for them to do to reach His people. And He has a purpose for you as well. In fact, it's a dual responsibility!

Questions to ponder or discuss with others:

1. What is it about a life of faith that keeps demanding of us greater testing, deeper searching, and more dependence?
2. Why is it that God can be so real, so personal, and so present with us? Then, at other times, seem to be so distant and so silent?
3. Does God use His silence to activate your faith?
4. Do you expect God to treat you differently than He did Abraham?
5. Has God used a time of silence in your life to rid you of some of your dross? To make you more pliable in His hands?
6. Can God's silence be used as a tool to activate your conscience?
7. God's silence in Joseph's life, David's life, and Job's life all produced patience and demonstrated in them a quality of genuineness. Is it possible that His silence in your life is for the same purpose?
8. Do you believe that God's silence is a part of His grace that He uses to draw you to Him?

Chapter 10

The Dual Responsibility

Their sound has gone out to all the earth,
And their words to the ends of the world.

—Romans 10:18

Wherever Jesus went, He took a mirror with Him. And as He met with people, He held that mirror up to them and let them see the backpack of preeminence they were carrying around. Nicodemus became aware of his empty religious pride.[1] The woman at the well had to face her shame.[2] The nobleman at Capernaum realized what a skeptic he was.[3] And the rich, young ruler came face-to-face with his deep self-centeredness.[4]

As they gazed into the raw reflection of who they really were—their reality—Jesus offered them the naked gospel. He offered to help them take off their heavy packs and to cut their puppet strings. He offered them His hand and a straight path through the mazes of life. It was a great offer—and a free one at that! You would think that

---

1. See John 3:1–21.
2. See John 4:4–30.
3. See John 4:43–54.
4. See Luke 18:18–23.

everyone to whom Jesus offered such an opportunity would jump at it, wouldn't you?

But Jesus got mixed responses. On one hand, were those who openly disdained God and anything related to Him. They pretended to ignore the mirror. On the other hand, were the religionists of the day—conservative, liberal, and everything in between. They wanted to believe that their reflections were different than what Jesus' mirror revealed to them and that they had no pack to come to terms with. They scoffed at both the mirror and the offer and denied its relevance to their lives. And many of them didn't stop at that. They aggressively waged war against the One who held up that mirror.

Only a few were willing to admit that what they saw in the mirror was accurate and to accept the responsibility. *Responsibility?* you may be wondering. *I thought salvation was free. What do you mean by* responsibility?

Yes, salvation is free. You can never earn it, merit it, or generate it. We are absolutely dependent on God's mercy to save the undeserving rebels that we are.[5]

But just because salvation is a gift doesn't mean that you can be careless with it. When I visit my grandchildren, they often give me gifts of their latest artwork: crayon-colored pictures or pencil sketches of stick men. I don't toss these gifts aside. I take them home and stick them to my refrigerator. When the grandchildren come to visit me, they see that I value their gifts—that I handle them responsibly.

Free—with conditions

Just so, the naked gospel is a free gift, but it is not without conditions.[6] The conditions are simple: Live it and give it. Accept it and share it. Apply it and communicate it. Open the gift—and then pass it around. That's the dual responsibility. Trying to embrace one without the other is a farce. Both elements go together.[7]

That's why Jesus' first missionaries were such an assorted bunch: demoniacs, a harlot, tax collectors, lepers, fishermen, and someone with a PhD. When each looked into that mirror and saw the pack of preeminence on his or her back, Jesus gave each a step to take that would deal with the issue of who is in charge. When the individual took that step, he or she then had a living testimony to share. That's evangelism. That's true missionary work. That's the dual responsibility: dealing with the pack of preeminence on your own back and then

---

5. See Ephesians 2:8, 9.
6. See 1 John 1:6, 7; Matthew 24:14.
7. See Matthew 5:16; James 1:27; Revelation 12:11.

sharing with others what God has done, and is doing, for you. The dual responsibility is appropriating the gospel and then propagating it. It's demonstrating it and then proclaiming it.

These two elements are as inseparable in the true Christian life as are hydrogen and oxygen in water. When we take the name *Christian,* we are accepting a dual responsibility, and we are accountable to God for the way we handle it.

To attempt to enjoy the benefits of the gospel without letting it flow out of your life to touch others is impossible. You will become stagnant and salty, like the Dead Sea that receives but never gives. You cannot be a fresh, sweet body of water without letting the blessings flow out beyond you. On the other hand, pretending you have the gospel and proclaiming it far and near, while your pack of preeminence remains undealt with, insults Christ and actually turns others away from the true experience of walking with God. It's offering polluted water to others, and it actually instills in them a distaste for the real thing.

That's why Gandhi said, "I like your Christ, but I do not like your Christians. Your Christians are so unlike your Christ."

What was Gandhi really saying? He was saying, I like what your Christ stands for. I like His principles and life. His words and actions matched! However, I don't see His followers living what Christ taught. Is Gandhi's analysis correct? Is there a great disparity between what we believe and profess and what we daily live?

Remember, Gandhi was a Hindu who had experienced extreme oppression from "Christian" governments in both South Africa and India. He knew that Christians professed to follow Christ, and he knew that Christ said, "No one can serve two masters; for either he will hate the one and love the other, or else he will be loyal to the one and despise the other. You cannot serve God and mammon."[8] And yet, time and time again, Gandhi saw that greed and materialism in "Christians" lead to the cruel degradation and criminal neglect of those whom they judged to be inferior to themselves.

This kind of witness stinks! And yet it continues on a smaller scale, day in and day out, among those who profess Christ, yet who are insensitive to their spouses and treat their children with indifference. We put on a "Christian" face with the people we rub shoulders with at work, in the community, and at church, but when we come under trial, stress, disappointment, heartache, or frenemy fire, what kind of fruit do they see in our lives? The sweet fruits of the Spirit? Or are we more like lemons: sour, sarcastic, and vehement?

Gandhi saw very clearly that there is often a huge disconnect between what

---

8. Matthew 6:24.

we profess and what we actually live. Ouch! As a Christian, that smarts. Why? Because it's true. It gets right to the core of the issue.

Dealing with the disconnect

The core of the issue is that we often give Christ the cold shoulder. Maybe our past experiences have led us to fear Him, hate Him, or simply not perceive Him. The way to that dusty, narrow old door where He stands knocking has often been piled high with obstructions until it seems very complicated to find Him.

Often, we simply don't like what we see in His mirror, and so we resist Him, avoid Him, and go it on our own. We substitute pure doctrine for a pure heart; correct lifestyle for correct motivation; and dead works for a living experience. We tie plastic fruit onto a lifeless tree and then zealously try to get others to do the same.

We seem to think that if we can get enough people doing what we're doing, then we are successful Christians. We sell them our church, our doctrines, our lifestyle, and our reforms. We make them into disciples of ourselves rather than into disciples of Christ. And all the while, Christ is bleeding because we have put Him in a corner. We give Him lip service, while our hearts are far from Him.[9]

In this, we fail in the dual responsibility. Not only have we put the cart before the horse, but we have left the horse in the stall, while we try to push the cart to the heavenly kingdom in our own strength. That cart contains some precious goods that need to be delivered to the world—solid biblical teaching, a wholesome lifestyle, and a church fellowship that doesn't bow to ungodly fads, practices, and teachings. But we need the horse to pull the cart!

A horse in the Bible represents victory, conquest, and strength.[10] In Revelation 19:11–14, Christ appears on a white horse, leading the armies of heaven. He is King of kings and Lord of lords. He is the only One who can heal the disconnect between what we profess and what we actually live. He is the only One who can generate life in the root of the dead tree and cause it to put forth green shoots and juicy, nourishing fruit. He is the only One who can give us a pure heart out of which flows our doctrines and lifestyle. Christ living in you and me is our only hope of glory![11] This transforming, vibrant, growing experience is the horse.

We must put this horse before the cart, not just in theory, but also in reality. Christ's words, His ways, His motivations, His heart must become our own.

---

9. See Isaiah 29:13.
10. See Revelation 6:2; Psalm 20:7; Jeremiah 4:13.
11. See Colossians 1:27.

Listening to Him, trusting Him, following Him must become our life. Jesus said, "Apart from me, you can do nothing." However, the apostle Paul said, "I can do all things through Christ who strengthens me."[12]

When we take Christ out of the corner of our lives and make Him our all, He will empower us to deal with our packs of preeminence so that we can possess a conscience void of offense before God and man. More than that, He links His strength with our weakness, His wisdom with our ignorance, and His presence with our isolation so that we become a living power for good. We become people of whom it can be said, "They love God with every fiber of their being and their neighbor as themselves." This is taking the horse out of the stall and hitching it to the cart.

Do you have the cart hitched to the horse? Don't leave the barn until it is. Jesus instructed, "Tarry ye . . . until ye be endued with power from on high."[13] Don't run ahead of God. Make sure you are getting your marching orders from Him. God's plans are often quite different from ours.

If I had been in charge of Jesus' life, I would have started Him in His public ministry when He was twelve years old. He knew the Scriptures so well that His probing questions confused the most learned men in the nation. He comprehended the meaning of the sacrificial services, while the vast majority of His countrymen went through the ceremonies with little perception of their significance. And He discerned His life mission. He knew He was the Son of God incarnate.

In my estimation, it was a waste of time and resources to send Him back to Nazareth at that point. Think of all the people He could have healed during the eighteen quiet years He spent at home. Think of all the sermons He could have preached that would have lifted the fog of ignorance from the minds of so many. Think of all the foreign nations He could have visited with the gospel.

But He followed God's timing for His life. He kept the horse before the cart. He went back to Nazareth and lived the quiet life of an ordinary citizen. He was faithful in His home duties and business. He served the little needs of his family members and neighbors. He lived an unselfish, unnoticed, and unapplauded life that developed a depth of character we hardly think possible. Because He was faithful in that which was least, He was able to be faithful under the greatest pressure and face the most discouraging odds anyone has ever confronted. Because, in the obscurity of tiny Nazareth, He had learned to keep the horse before the cart, He could do so in the bright light of the world's scrutiny as well. He lived out true godliness.

12. John 15:5, NIV; Philippians 4:13.
13. Luke 24:49, KJV.

One of my favorite authors, a woman who lived near to God, wrote, "A revival of true godliness among us is the greatest and most urgent of all our needs. To seek this should be our first work."[14] This is hitching the cart to the horse. Don't leave the barn until this is accomplished.

And wherever the horse goes, the cart is sure to follow. The cart doesn't wait until the horse gets to the end of the journey before it starts out—and neither should your witness for Christ wait until you have a completely mature experience with Him. Your witness for Christ begins the moment He takes preeminence in your life. As quickly as He changes you, your world, your sphere of influence, will have a living testimony.

Who's waiting for whom?

Most Christians are waiting for some great end-time event to occur that will signal the end of the world and the second coming of Christ. They watch for a scenario involving a national Sunday law, Armageddon, an economic collapse, the antichrist, the Middle East, the beast power, or the king of the north versus the king of the south. They believe that when some combination of these events occurs, they just need to grit their teeth through the tough times and then go home to the kingdom.

Others are waiting for the promised "latter rain" of the Holy Spirit to transform them and enable them to do an amazing work that will turn the world upside down.

God is waiting, too, but He's not waiting for the same things many of us are. Simply put, He is waiting for *us*! "Christ is waiting with longing desire for the manifestation of Himself in His church."[15] That's the naked gospel. That's dealing with "the issue" and making Christ preeminent in our lives so that the same fruit that was seen in His life is seen in ours. "The fruit of the Spirit is love, joy, peace, longsuffering, gentleness, goodness, faith, meekness, temperance."[16]

If all of us who have taken the name *Christian* were bearing this kind of fruit, both privately and publicly, we'd have a lot of horse-drawn carts going everywhere with the naked gospel. The gospel commission would be finished, and Christ would come to claim His own. "When the fruit is brought forth, immediately he putteth in the sickle, because the harvest is come."[17]

---

14. Ellen White, *Selected Messages* (Washington, D.C.: Review and Herald® Publishing Association, 1958), book 1, 121.

15. Ellen White, *Christ's Object Lessons* (Mountain View, Calif.: Pacific Press®, 1900), 69.

16. Galatians 5:22, 23, KJV.

17. Mark 4:29, KJV.

The character of Christ is defined as living to love God with all that you are and to love your neighbors as yourself. And *when* this character is perfectly reproduced in His people, *then* He will come to claim them as His own.[18]

Please note the *when* and *then*. There is a cause-and-effect relationship implied here. God is waiting for His character to be reproduced in you as you relate to your spouse and children, as you interact in your workplace and at church, as you mingle with your neighbors or people at the store, and as you come across opportunities to help those in far-off places. He is waiting for His values to shape your appetites, recreations, objectives, habits, uses of time, entertainment, work, and home life. He is waiting to become your all. I'd say knowing the *who* takes precedence over knowing the *when*!

Is God waiting on you? Yes or no? May He wait no more!

Ray and Becky

Ray and Becky are finding the power of the naked gospel. They were caught in an endless downward spiral of alcohol and arguing. Daily, they threatened each other with divorce. They felt locked in despair with no way out. But God had His eye on them and purposed to bring them hope.

Sam was the attorney for the construction company that both Ray and Becky worked for. He hired Ray and Becky for some of his own construction projects. While working on Sam's house, Ray noticed his interaction with his wife and children. He had never seen a man treat his family so well before.

Ray and Becky hit rock bottom when she ended up in jail for public intoxication. Becky needed an attorney, but she avoided calling Sam. She was embarrassed and afraid that Sam wouldn't want to work with them. But all the other attorneys Becky called didn't work out. Finally, she called Sam. To her grateful surprise, he was sympathetic and gave her the assistance she needed without shaming her.

As Sam and Becky were talking about her situation, she expressed a desire for a better life. That's when Sam told her about a camp meeting. At first, Ray and Becky wanted to go, but then realized they couldn't afford it. When Sam offered to pay their expenses, Ray and Becky recognized that they were also afraid of taking this step. Would they like the camp meeting? Would the people there accept them? Finally, their longings outweighed their fears, and they decided to go.

As they listened during meeting after meeting, the Holy Spirit worked a miracle in their hearts—instilling hope in place of despair. They saw that God

---

18. See Ellen White, *Christ's Object Lessons,* 69.

had a better way for them and that He was willing to take them by the hand and empower them to live in a better way.

As Ray and Becky drove home, they wrote down the changes they planned to make—stop smoking, drinking, partying, and arguing, replacing those things with pure air, clean water, Bible study, and prayer. (By the way, no one at the camp meeting had said anything to them about any of these specific items. They were simply responding to the leading of the Holy Spirit!) They followed through. God removed their cravings for alcohol and enabled them to express affection for each other rather than anger. As they studied their Bibles by themselves and with Sam's family, they made more changes. They began to keep the Sabbath. Hope was restored; a new life has entered their life. They are now working out what God is working in.

Their lives are becoming a living demonstration of the gospel of Jesus Christ. They have found a power, and they are making it theirs. They are letting it liberate them. They are letting it revitalize their marriage. They are letting it reconnect them to the Vine. Now they've got something! They've got a living demonstration of God's power.

How about you? Is your life, marriage, family, and church a living witness of the power of God? It can be when you learn to walk with Him daily. Ray and Becky now have a "proclamation" to make to all whom they come in contact with.

Oh, how I wish Gandhi could have met this couple!

Proclamation

You and I have a dual responsibility. It is to demonstrate the power of the gospel in our daily lives and then to proclaim this living gospel to the unreached. We must come to see that we need both a demonstration and a proclamation and that the proclamation naturally flows from a living demonstration.

"Their sound has gone out to all the earth, and their words to the ends of the world."[19] Your "sound" is a proclamation that resonates from your life's witness. In other words, your *life* speaks so loudly, I want to *hear* your words. Tell me more! Proclaim it. For what I see, I want to be.

People didn't follow Jesus because He spoke the truth. They followed Jesus because He *lived* the truth He spoke. The temple officers who were sent to spy on Jesus came back with the report that never had a man spoken as He spoke.[20] But the reason for this was that never had a man lived as He lived. Had His life

---

19. Romans 10:18.
20. See John 7:45–47.

been other than it was, He could not have spoken as He did. There was a "sound" that spoke louder than His words. His words and His sound matched. They were identical.

Consider this question: If you were to ask your spouse, children, or closest acquaintances what sound you make, and if they were to answer honestly, what would they say? Would they say you make a harmonious sound? Out of tune? Discordant? Does your sound match your words? Go ahead and get a consensus. If you are reluctant to do so, why do you think that is? Perhaps you already have your answer.

Why do I challenge you to look at your fruit before sharing your juice? Because Jesus said, "By their fruits ye shall know them."[21] This is your sound.

Paul said, "Examine yourselves, whether ye be in the faith."[22] In other words, what is your sound? Are you a genuine Christian? Are you in tune with Christ? If so, play it and proclaim it! If not, retune, regroup, and find the sound God designed you to produce.

Ray and Becky have a new sound—a new song to sing. No, they are not a philharmonic orchestra. No, they don't know the entire song yet. But their duet is worth hearing. Why? Because the part of the song they know, they are singing. They are sincere and honest in their current experience!

I remember going to a children's violin recital. The twelve-year-old daughter of a friend was performing in it. When she got to the end of her piece, everyone—and I mean, everyone—applauded! Why? It wasn't because her performance was flawless, because it wasn't. It was because her performance was perfect for her level of musical development. *Her sound was in tune for where she was and what she knew!*

Are you in tune for where you are and what you know? If you are, then God says that your words are to go to the ends of the world.[23] Those words conjure up a picture in my mind of a pouring forth—a proclamation. That "pouring forth" is giving yourself to help others find what you have found— the naked gospel that connects you with an authentic walk with God, that brings a fresh element into your marriage, that rejuvenates your family, and that simplifies your life to make room for real priorities.

Whatever your present testimony is, proclaim it!

The demoniacs were liberated and proclaimed it.

The harlot was cleansed and proclaimed it.

The tax collector was forgiven and proclaimed it.

---

21. Matthew 7:20, KJV.
22. 2 Corinthians 13:5, KJV.
23. See Romans 10:18; Matthew 24:14.

The nobleman's son was healed and proclaimed it.

The man with the PhD was cured of his spiritual blindness and proclaimed it.

What is your present testimony? Do you have something to proclaim? Revelation 12:11 says that "they overcame him by the blood of the Lamb and by the word of their testimony." Do you see the dual responsibility here? When you overcome your pack of preeminence with the blood of the Lamb, you have a testimony to share, and it is vital that you share it. The word of your testimony can help to defeat the devil's encroachment into other's lives. They need to hear and see a living demonstration of the power of the gospel.

Ray and Becky's present testimony says, "The devil of alcohol, tobacco, video mania, harsh words, and divorce threats no longer controls us!"

That's the power of the gospel. They have a proclamation. They are being liberated, changed, and transformed. They are like a seedling popping up its head and growing in the warmth of the "Son" as a result of its death experience in the earth. If Ray and Becky continue the growth process, they will mature into sturdy stalks, which will develop ears of corn that will ripen until harvest.[24]

At each stage, from seedling to full maturity, their testimony will bear evidence that God is real, that God is there, that God lives, and that God's grace is supreme in their lives. At each stage, God will have a testimony for them to bear and a work for them to embrace—not in word only, but also in sound! These two are inseparably one. They were inseparable in Jesus' life. They are to be inseparable in our lives as well.

Pure religion

You see, we need to thoughtfully evaluate which class of responders we fall into when Christ holds up that mirror before us. According to James, some take a look and go their way, trying to forget what they saw. They are "hearer[s] of the word," but not doers of the word.[25]

Others continue to gaze into that mirror and then pick up the work of dealing with what they see. They are not forgetful hearers. They are doers. They act on the word and pick up the dual responsibility.[26]

Their religion is expressed in practical personal living. It is carried out in their everyday lives. It touches not only those closest to them, but also reaches to the unfortunate ones in the world.

James expressed it like this: "Pure religion and undefiled religion before

---

24. See Mark 4:28.
25. James 1:23, 24.
26. See James 1:25.

God and the Father is this." "This" means *listen up!* "This" is the summation. And what does James say constitutes pure, undefiled religion? "To visit orphans and widows in their trouble, and to keep oneself unspotted from the world."[27]

Orphans and widows! Why did James say "orphans and widows"? Because they cannot reciprocate. This is a test of motive. Why do you give? Why do you help? When you freely share from the abundance with which God has blessed you—without looking for brownie points, paybacks, or perks—you are reflecting God's character.

Scripture says that God is committed to caring for the powerless and defenseless, including the poor, the alien, the fatherless, and the widow. Since the needs of such people are on God's heart, He expects that same heart to be in us. Further, Jesus so identified Himself with needy, oppressed people that when we care for one of His people in need, we do it unto Him.[28] To close our hearts to suffering and need is to close our hearts to Christ.

But "orphans and widows" means more than just literal orphans and widows. They are symbolic of the true needs of *all* people whoever they are. Ministering to those with needs may mean

- taking a loaf of bread to your neighbor
- building a church in the Congo
- visiting a prisoner
- giving a Bible study
- handing out a book
- sharing a video or CD
- bringing someone to a meeting
- selling all your surplus to aid the unfortunate
- changing careers to minister full time
- accepting a position in your local church
- challenging the worldliness in your church, denomination, or group
- homeschooling your children
- simplifying your life in order to have time for the true priorities of life
- babysitting your grandchildren or great-grandchildren
- full-time or part-time evangelism
- writing a book
- giving your testimony

---

27. James 1:27.
28. See Matthew 25:40.

Pure religion is a giving of yourself, your talents, your assets, and your heart to God's cause as *He* impresses you to do. You can't do everything on that list all of the time; we are finite beings. But are our hearts utterly disposed to do all the good we can within the limits of our finiteness, trusting God with the ripple effect? A pebble dropped in the ocean disappears quickly, but the ripple it creates continues long after its initial splash is gone.

If you want to walk with God, you must walk where He walks. Not in silence only, but also in service. God walks not only in the places of natural beauty that quiet our senses and bring peace to our souls. He also walks in the slums of the world's big cities, in your neighbor's house, in the jungle huts where spiritualism thrives, and in your children's bedrooms. He walks the streets of your town and sits in the pews of your church. Everywhere human needs exist—that is where Christ walks. And to walk with Him, you must be willing to work alongside Him to help and bless those that you can.

Pure religion is caring for the needy—whoever they are, wherever they are, whenever God calls, however often God calls—and maintaining personal holiness before, during, and after His call![29]

There's the dual responsibility: dealing with your own heart and helping others. It's interesting to note the order in which James presents this dual responsibility. For James, outreach precedes "inreach." That's because contact with people is sure to awaken a realization of your own need for the naked gospel. This is one of the ways God holds up that mirror before us and shows us our packs of preeminence. We go back to the quiet place to deal with our own hearts and then re-engage in our work.

This keeps us in step with Christ. Jesus lived a constant cycle between the mountain and the multitude, the monastery and the mission. If we are to be laborers together with Him, we must follow Him in both aspects of life. Following Him in service heightens your awareness of your need for Him in silence. And times of quiet communion with Him inspire you to minister to the needs of those about you. One without the other is dead. Combining both brings vitality to your experience.

Let your light shine!

In 1977 Paul and Ethel Conner opened our eyes to the Scriptures. Wow! Our lives have never been the same. As Sally and I look back on it, we see a three-step pattern repeating itself over and over. God brings us truth, helps us apply it to our experience, and then gives us opportunities to share it.

My priest, parents, siblings, and close friends heard a "word" from me within

---

29. James 1:27.

days of my opening the Bible for the first time in my life. A light had been lit in my life, and God says, "Neither do [men] light a lamp, and put it under the bushel, but on the stand; and it shineth unto all that are in the house."[30] There's the dual responsibility again! Light the lamp and then let it shine on everyone in the house!

I believe that "unto all that are in the house" means to all with whom you have an influence. In those early days, I put up a rack of free Christian literature in my insurance office and encouraged all my clients to take whatever caught their attention. That "proclamation" led to nearly a dozen baptisms over the next couple of years.

How are you using the influence God has given you? Seriously! We each need to take an honest inventory of our influence and how God would have us use it.

In the thirty-three years since that first Bible study Sally and I took, God has tuned our sound and broadened our word.[31] As we found God real and present in our lives, our desire expanded to touch others with that which had touched us.

God has used us as His "mailmen" to deliver love letters to His people. It started very small—sharing our personal testimony with a few people—and has grown to a speaking ministry that has taken us throughout the United States, Canada, and Mexico to South America, Europe, Australia, New Zealand, and Africa. Our speaking messages have developed into thirteen books, sixteen booklets, thirty-six CD sets, and fourteen DVD sets that have gone out to more than twenty countries around the world.

Why us? Why has our influence spread so far beyond our first dreams? Is our flesh and blood somehow different than yours? Does God play favorites? Not at all. It's been our willingness to allow Him to be the preeminent One all along the way!

What He has done for us, in us, and through us, He wants to do with everyone. He wants to deliver a message to His people through you. He wants to make a mailman out of you! Will you let Him? Will you cooperate with Him? It may be as simple as what my two sons are doing.

Matthew keeps several of my books sitting on his desk in his office. *Escape to God* draws the majority of questions. Matthew explains, "This is how I was raised. This is what I believe!" He offers a copy to all who are interested.

Sally and I were taking an evening walk down our mountain road when a man stopped his vehicle, rolled down his window, and called to us by name.

---

30. Matthew 5:15, ASV; brackets in original.
31. To read more of our story, see my first book, *Escape to God.*

"You must be Jim and Sally Hohnberger!"

I looked closely at the man as I walked up to his window. "I'm sorry, sir. Have we met?"

"Your son, Andrew, sold me some property and gave me your book *Come to the Quiet*."

Andrew is not ashamed of his father or his father's beliefs. Is that you? Are you ashamed of your heavenly Father or His beliefs? If not, then let your light shine, so that you may glorify—not you or your church—but your Father which is in heaven![32]

Let your sound pour forth

Can you imagine what this world would be like if every Christian picked up the dual responsibility? What would it be like if everyone played out his or her part in word and sound? What would happen if you and I, with our sons and daughters, cooperated with God in saving others and bringing them back to Him?

Together, we would form an orchestra whose sound would be heard to the ends of the earth. Of course, you know that an orchestra is made up of various instruments—strings, winds, brass, and percussion. They each have their own unique sound and their own unique part to play. The oboe's musical score is very different from the cello's. The trumpet does not attempt to play the part of the flute. If each played when and what they wanted to play, the sound would be bedlam, a discordant, ear-splitting noise. But when they individually follow the signals of the conductor and play the unique score he has assigned them, their sounds become part of a symphony!

God wants to conduct His people as they play the symphony of the naked gospel for Gandhi—and for every nation, kindred, tongue, and people. He wants this symphony to invite them to know, see, and experience for themselves what it means to walk with God.

You can't be that entire orchestra, but you can be one instrument. You have a unique sound and a unique part to play that is unlike any other. You can tune your sound to God. You can make sure you are following the Conductor, regardless of what others around you are doing. You can walk in your integrity.

---

32. See Matthew 5:16.

Questions to ponder or discuss with others:

1. Was Gandhi's perception right: "I like your Christ, I don't like your Christians"?
2. What was Gandhi really saying?
3. Is there a great disparity in your life?
4. Is "a revival of true godliness among us" truly the greatest and most urgent of our needs?
5. If so, should seeking this be our first work?
6. What does God mean when He says, "Tarry ye . . . until ye be endued with power from on high"?
7. Have you really learned to walk with God daily?
8. Are your life, marriage, and family living demonstrations of the power of the gospel?
9. Is God waiting on a Sunday law or is He waiting for His people?
10. Are you proclaiming both the sound and the words He has given you?
11. Are you honestly using your influence to reach the unreached around you?
12. Who and where are the "orphans and widows" whom God is asking you to reach out and touch?
13. Is God asking you to deliver His "mail"?
14. Does God want to use you to reach the nations?
15. Are you tuning your sound to God and following the directions of the Conductor?

Chapter 11

Walk in Your Integrity

But as for me, I will walk in my integrity;
Redeem me and be merciful to me.

—Psalm 26:11

O ne of my all-time favorite stories was written by Patricia McGerr back
in 1965 and produced as a short film in 1969.[1]

In the story, Johnny Lingo, an astute Polynesian trader, has come
to a primitive village in the South Pacific islands to bargain for a wife.
Everyone, even her father, considers Mahana, the young woman
Johnny desires, to be of little value. Sullen, unkempt, and ashamed, she
creeps around the village with her shoulders hunched, avoiding contact with people whenever possible.

The going rate for a fair-to-middling wife is two or three cows.
Four or five would buy a highly satisfactory wife. A counselor advised
Mahana's father, Moke, to ask for three cows, so that when the bar-
gaining ended, he would get at least one.

Of course, the bargaining is a public event attended by the entire

1. Wikipedia, "LDS movies," Wikipedia, http://en.wikipedia.org/w/
index.php?title=LDS_movies&oldid=355419710 (accessed April 26, 2010).

village. Who would miss such entertainment? As the bargaining is about to begin, the women of the island brag to each other about how many cows their husbands had given for each of them and comment that Mahana's father will be lucky if Lingo offers even one cow.

The bargaining begins and, as the counselor suggested, Moke asks Johnny Lingo for three cows. The villagers think that's terribly funny and break into derisive laughter.

Lingo raises his hand to silence the uproar and then makes his counteroffer. "Three cows are many," he states deliberately, "but not enough for my Mahana!" He then offers the unheard-of price of eight cows for Mahana's hand in marriage.

The next day, the villagers gather at the house of Mahana's father to see the deal completed. Some of the islanders are saying that Lingo will reconsider his offer and not show up. But Lingo brings the eight cows. He and Mahana then leave the island on a honeymoon.

When they come back, a shopkeeper pays a visit to their hut—partly for business and partly out of curiosity. He discovers, to his astonishment, that Mahana is a beautiful, happy woman, aglow with confidence and affection for her husband. The transformation is so remarkable to everyone, that even Mahana's father begins accusing Johnny Lingo of cheating him by giving only eight cows for a girl truly worth ten. Johnny, Mahana's proud husband, had proved to her that her true worth had nothing to do with what others saw, but rather with what she truly was and could be—if nurtured and cherished.[2]

I love the way the story illustrates the impact our treatment of others can have on them. But even more than that, I love the allegory that I see in the story of my own life. You see, I was Mahana.

Hiding in shame

I spent the first thirty days of kindergarten under my teacher's desk! I was timid, shy, and terrified. Mrs. Pritchard must have had a real mother's heart. She didn't jerk me out by the arm and plop me down in my own desk. She waited, hoping my fears would melt in the warmth of all the interesting activities going on. But after a month with no change, she pinned a note to my shirt for my mother.

The next day, my mother accompanied me to school. As long as she sat beside me at my desk, I was fine. So the following day, Mother sent me to school by myself again, hoping that now that the ice was broken, so to speak, I'd be ready to get into the activities like the other kids. But that wasn't how I felt. I just had an overwhelming urge to hide.

---

2. See ibid.

I sensed that Mrs. Pritchard wasn't going to be quite so lenient with me any-more, so I took the next best way out. I played hooky! That's right—in kinder-garten, I skipped school! I stood under a tree on a hill between school and home that morning and just watched the activity on the street. When I heard the bell ring, I figured school was over for the day and went home. I didn't realize that it was only the noon-hour bell—not the bell at the end of the school day!

I walked in the back door and called out, "Hi, Mom!"

My mother glanced at the clock and asked, "How was school, Jimmy?" From my answer, she figured out pretty quickly what was going on, and I didn't get away with ditching school or hiding under the teacher's desk anymore.

But although my body was sitting in my assigned chair, my heart was still under the teacher's desk. That shameful desire to hide remained. I felt so infe-rior to the other kids. I didn't seem to have any natural abilities. I wasn't tal-ented like some of them. I was just me. Simple, plain Jimmy.

I didn't know it then, but I can look back now and see how God was there, working in my life. He knew the person He had created me to be and put into place His plan to walk hand in hand with little old me.

Broken integrity

In the words of Solomon, "God made man upright."[3] He made him to walk with his head high, his conscience clear, and his self-respect intact. He made him to own his thoughts, his values, and his choices. He made him to sail his own seas with a rudder that would cut a straight course through contrary winds and tides. He made him to love boldly, to create uniquely, and to bear the impress of God's own image. In short, He made him to walk in integrity. Integrity is living in the unimpaired state of being the person God created you to be!

When God formed Adam from the dust of the ground and breathed into his nostrils the breath of life, He never intended Adam to become a puppet danc-ing to the tune of someone else's pipe.

But Adam turned from his high calling. He sold his birthright for a pittance, and his integrity was broken. In trying to gain something God had supposedly withheld, in cowering to the fear of losing Eve, in dodging the responsibility for his own choice, Adam forfeited his God-given individuality and opened the way for the master of puppets to tie up all of us in strings.

The devil is like Moke—except he is a lot more deliberate in his designs to keep us dumbed down. He rules us through self-condemning thoughts, pride-ful attitudes, and creeping fears. He keeps us running in circles through empty

---

3. Ecclesiastes 7:29.

mazes, loaded down with heavy packs. He does his best to defeat us with shame or overwhelm us with pride—anything that will keep us from our true legacy, the experience of walking in our integrity.

But God does not abandon us. He still sees value in us. Michelangelo, the famous sculptor, once said, "I saw an angel in the block of marble, and I just chiseled until I set him free." That's how God is. He sees the possibilities He Himself has implanted within every son and daughter of Adam, and He works through the avenues of our lives to chisel away all that keeps us from our destiny.

God could see a king in the no-count shepherd boy from Judah.[4] He could see a great missionary in the voracious persecutor of the early Christian church.[5] He could see John the beloved in the impetuous "Son of Thunder."[6] He saw the deliverer of His people in a pagan Persian king.[7] He saw the mother of His own Son in a young peasant girl.[8]

God also sees possibilities in those who turn their backs on Him. Who might Judas have become if he had submitted to God's chiseling process? What might Solomon have been had he held fast to his integrity from the beginning of his life? What legacy might Jezebel have bequeathed to God's people had she made Him preeminent?

God sees in us the potential for a beauty and strength beyond our wildest dreams. And He is willing to keep chipping away at the marble until the real man or woman in us emerges. He is our Creator. He is our Redeemer. He paid a price for us far exceeding eight cows because He wants us to value ourselves accordingly. He risked eternal loss and separation so that you and I might have the chance to know what it means to walk in integrity.

God is at work in the life of every individual, whether they acknowledge Him or not. He is at work in your life, whether or not you are a professing or practicing Christian. He is at work in the life of your atheist friend and your agnostic neighbor. He was at work in my life—even when I was pleading with the cold statue of Mary and playing casually with Ouija boards. To the extent that I cooperated with the voice of my conscience, God was able to take me to the next step of reclaiming the integrity He created me to have.

Who I am today is the result of God believing in the possibilities He Himself had implanted within me and of my responding to His calls to my heart.

---

4. See 1 Samuel 16:1, 7.
5. See Acts 9:15.
6. Mark 3:17.
7. See Isaiah 44:28; 45:1.
8. See Luke 1:26–38.

Own your own life

As I've mentioned already, I try to take what I call my "Enoch time" each year. I put on my backpack and head up to a remote mountain lake to be alone with God. What do I do there? I listen! I listen to God speaking through His Word. I listen to Him through the wonders of the natural world around me. And I listen to God whispering to my conscience.

I've read that "the silence of the soul makes more distinct the voice of God."[9] That's why the devil has the whole world on a treadmill pace and constantly bombards our minds. He is all too successful at jamming the frequencies between God and us so that God's whispers to our conscience are drowned out.

One recent outing was particularly memorable. I climbed the rocky ridge behind my campsite and settled down to rest on an inviting-looking boulder. My eyes feasted on the sparkling sapphire lake below me, the wildflowers that dotted the green meadows, and the mighty snowcapped peaks rising all around me. A familiar song rose in my heart, "This Is My Father's World."

As I sat there pondering the majesty of God and His working in my life, He whispered to me, *"Jim, own your own life. Don't be afraid to be the person I've called you to be. Don't merely blend into the thinking of the day and times you live in. Don't just play out a role someone else assigns to you. Be faithful in what I have called you to. Live authentically, according to the principles you have internalized from My Word. Walk in your integrity."*

Then God stirred some memories of my past and showed me how He had been at work all through my life to cut the devil's puppet strings and to restore me to His original design for me. You see, some people who first meet me think I've always been comfortable in public ministry—speaking, writing, and counseling. Nothing could be further from the truth. In a lot of ways, I would probably still be hiding under the teacher's desk had not God been my Johnny Lingo. Of course, the process He's brought me through has taken a lifetime— and He's not done with me yet!

Peer pressure

The first memory God brought to my mind was the intense peer pressure I experienced during my school years. Peer pressure is the expectation others put on us or that we put on ourselves to be just like those around us, so that we can feel accepted. Back in those days, I wanted so badly to be liked, to fit in, and to belong. Most of us have those desires, and they are not wrong in and of them-selves unless they lead us to lower our standards or compromise God's principles.

---

9. Ellen White, *The Ministry of Healing* (Mountain View, Calif.: Pacific Press®, 1942), 58.

When our need for belonging undermines our high calling, we have a problem!

Why? Because it's allowing other people to be preeminent over our lives. There will always be people, or groups of people, who want to assign us roles to play. These could be our friends, our relatives, our employers—even our church or our society. These people want to tell us how to talk, how to dress, how to eat and drink, how to spend our leisure time, and even how to worship. Sometimes they wrinkle up their noses and point their fingers at us when we don't do things the way they expect us to, and we feel pressure—peer pressure.

The next time you're feeling that pressure, remember that if Jesus had succumbed to peer pressure, there would have been no hope for the human race. Jesus couldn't be just like "them." He had to be the Person His Father called Him to be. He had to walk in His integrity.[10]

Jesus lived by two principles: First, He loved His Father with every fiber of His being and was zealous to honor Him in all things. Second, He loved us enough to seek to rescue us. These two principles were like a ship's rudder that steered Him through the intense pressure to conform that His peers placed on Him. But He was true to His purpose and true to His principles. He walked in integrity.

God has a purpose for your life that no one else can fulfill. No, none of us is the Savior of the world. But we each have our place in the web of humanity. God designs that we shall be living forces for righteousness in our own spheres. We cannot be that if we are controlled by peer pressure. We must base our life on principle and allow the Holy Spirit to be our daily Guide. This is what it means to walk in integrity. Finding this walk is not easy—but it is essential and life changing. Discovering the real *you*—the individual God designed *you* to be—is a must for all of us!

Who are you?

What dictates the style of your clothing? Is it the latest fad? Is it what your friends, peers, or the "in crowd" are wearing? Is it what comes out of Hollywood or Nashville? Who or what is the deciding factor or the driving force?

My heart goes out to our youth today. They've got rings in their ears, rings in their noses, and rings in their tongues. The more "undressed" or sloppy they look, the cooler they think they are. Shoes, shirt, blouse, pants, skirts, and socks—nothing coordinates, fits, or blends. Some of them have tattoos all over their bodies.

In their attempt to avoid conforming to "traditional" standards of dress, they are sacrificing their uniqueness on the altar of fashion. In the effort to fit in and belong, they are missing their own individual integrity. Most of them don't

---

10. See Proverbs 19:1; 20:7.

realize who is leading and influencing them.

I understand what they're dealing with because this was a difficult issue for me to deal with—especially in my teen years. Why? Because peer pressure pulled me in one direction, while that voice to my conscience kept calling me to a different standard.

My peers thought it was cool to not look their best, I disagree. I feel that one should always look his or her best. Yes, clothing should be appropriate for the occasion. You don't dress up for church when you're headed to the park. But there is never a time when it is not appropriate to be clean, well groomed, and to wear well-fitting, nicely matched clothing. I didn't understand it then, but now I know it is God's standard for me—for my life! This conviction began to crystallize for me in junior high school and has stayed with me through the years.

I'm not trying to make dress style a point of integrity for you. Maybe God is placing on your heart a completely different issue related to peer pressure. However, I've had to wrestle for decades with the fact that God has called me to a different standard, both in outward dress and inward integrity, than what I see all about me.

Over and over again, the question I have had to face is, Will I walk in my integrity and please God? Or will I bow to the whims of fashion, fads, peers, and society?

Some have said to me, "Jim, it's a little thing. Relax. Ease up. Let your hair down." But to me, it's a matter of personal integrity. It's living in the entire, unimpaired state of being the person God has called *me* to be!

A friend once told me, "A man who won't stand for something will fall for anything." Are you able to stand among your peers for what you really believe? Seriously! Or do you adjust, compromise, and lower your personal integrity?

Don't follow the buffalo

In Montana, where I live, huge herds of buffalo used to roam the plains. The Native Americans understood the habits of these animals and had a unique way of hunting them. The buffalo's migration patterns led them, at certain times of the year, to places where rolling prairies suddenly gave way to steep cliffs. Hunters systematically drove hundreds of buffalo over these cliffs, while other hunters waited at the bottom to dispatch the injured animals and begin butchering them.

This hunting technique was so successful because the buffalo instinctively pressed together as a herd when they felt threatened. Although this worked well for them in many situations, in this instance, following the crowd was a fatal mistake.

It seems to me that John the Baptist wasn't a buffalo when it came to his dress.[11] He did not follow the crowd. He dared to be the man *he* was called to be! He walked in his personal integrity!

My point is simple: Don't follow the buffalo! Don't follow John the Baptist! Don't follow Jim Hohnberger! Be the person *you* were born to be! *Own your own integrity!*

Ask God what His standards are for *you* in the areas of dress, music, diet, entertainment, recreation, education, or mission! Go ahead. Take some "Enoch time"—some time alone with God to hear what kind of person He's created you to be. No, you don't need to backpack to a wilderness lake like I do. (Although I think you are really missing something special if you don't!) Be creative for who *you* are! Find a cabin on a lake. Rent a condo on a beach. Borrow someone's cottage up north. Take a quiet room at Grandpa's or Grandma's place. Pitch a tent in your favorite campground. Hide out in your apartment. Whatever, wherever, however, do it! Do it for you! Do it for your God! Do it for your loved ones! But please do it! Let Him be the preeminent One for the person you are to be! Go ahead. Own your own life, then begin to sail your own seas.

Sail your own seas

When I graduated from college in 1972 with a degree in forestry land management, I could not find a job in my field of study. In fact, I was one of more than six hundred applicants for one particular position. Since I was a white male, the affirmative action program stacked the odds against me even more. I was so frustrated! What good is a college degree if you can't use it?

On a trip back to my hometown of Appleton, Wisconsin, I stopped by ABM Inc. to visit my brother. He was out of the office momentarily, and while I waited for him to return, I overheard the owner of the business expressing his frustration over a new minicomputer system he wanted to demo to a surveying company.

I stepped into the doorway of his office and smiled at him.

In his frustration, he looked up at me and blurted out, "Do you know anything about side shots?"

I smiled again and replied, "As a matter of fact, I have a minor in surveying. I think I could help you out."

He pulled up a chair for me, and I began to walk him through his dilemma. That opened up a dialogue over the next couple of weeks, which resulted in the company hiring me as its sales and marketing representative for engineering firms.

Six months later, the company was wrestling with whether to let me go or to cut my salary and expenses in half. I hadn't sold a thing! Not one computer!

---

11. See Matthew 3:4.

It wasn't that I hadn't given it the good old college try, I had! I had listened to all the sales and marketing tapes, imitated my brother's technique, and adopted my manager's style. I had approached all the bosses of all the engineering firms within my territory and had made good sales pitches. I had followed all the techniques I had been trained in. I did everything by the book. But I still had not managed to close even one sale.

Talk about being frustrated! I was ready to throw in the towel. To make quitting even more tempting, I was offered another position in line with my college major. Boy, was that intriguing!

But something within me said, "Jim, don't quit while you're failing. You can do it. Stick it out until you find *you!*"

Well, the company cut my salary and expense account in half. That did it. I threw in the towel—not regarding the job, but in terms of doing it their way. The way everyone else did sales might work for them, but it obviously was not working for me!

I ventured out to sail my own seas. Sometimes that's scary! Just ask Christopher Columbus. There's a great risk in proving the world is not flat. But there's also a great benefit to following your own heart, conscience, and integrity!

So I quit charting my course by everyone else's maps and followed my own intuition—an intuition I had been ignoring for months.

Crunching numbers

The next week, I stopped at a very large, reputable engineering firm. The surveying field crew had just come back to the office with a whole stack of numbers to crunch. They had to apply all their formulas by hand, using only a calculator with a square-root function. (Back in those days, this calculator was considered to be cutting-edge technology, but it was a monster that measured about eight inches by twelve inches and cost about six hundred dollars.)

My approach was to enter all their field data into my computer. Since I had a minor in surveying, I could speak their language. I asked for their points, bearings, distances, and angles. Then I pressed a button, and presto! Their surveys were balanced and closed. The process that they usually spent days completing was done in a matter of minutes—and with a smaller margin of error!

They were impressed! I didn't have to offer twice to teach them how to use my computer! I spent a full day training them, and when they were comfortable using the program, I left it with them for a week or two. When I went back to get my computer, they refused to let me have it. They could no longer live without it.

That one-day demonstration garnered me the largest sale at that point in the history of the company. I was now up and running, sailing my own seas, owning my own integrity. No longer would I try to sell in word only, but in demonstration also!

Using this approach, I started placing computers in all the engineering firms in northeast Wisconsin and the Upper Peninsula of Michigan. My sales and marketing career was on a high!

As I look back on it, I realize that my sales success came from being brave enough to walk in my own integrity. To stay locked in the fear of venturing into the unknown would have barred me from living in the entire, unimpaired state of what God called me to do and to be.

Each of us needs to examine our lives and ask some questions of ourselves. Am I walking in step with God's calling for *me*? Am I valuing the treasure of my uniqueness with which God has entrusted me? Do I cultivate my mind, heart, and soul in line with God's design for me? Am I ministering to others in the way God planned for me to do it?

God created a lot of different kinds of flowers, and He loves their uniqueness. He wants them to be all He made them to be and not try to be something different. A sunflower shouldn't try to smell like a rose. A pansy shouldn't tell a daffodil to arrange its petals like a pansy. The wild Indian paintbrush that grows so prolifically in the high mountain passes near our home would wilt in the steamy jungles of Brazil. Each flower is unique—and each meets the purpose of its creation when it blooms with all its heart the way it was meant to bloom, where it was meant to bloom, and when it was meant to bloom.

Different things hold us back. Often fear cripples us. Confusion cripples us. Unbelief in God cripples us. That's why God says, "Who can find a faithful man?"[12] God is not into cookie cutouts. He has only one of you, and that is the person you are to be! Listen to His call to your heart, reflect on the principles of His Word as they apply to your life, identify and face the fears that hold you back, and step out with Him to own your integrity!

Owning your integrity

After selling computers for some time, I eventually decided I wanted to own my own business. After a lot of research, I chose a multiline insurance agency that specialized in insurance for home, health, life, autos, and businesses.

When I first chose to sell insurance, I didn't realize that there are some lines that are extremely profitable and others that are not. However, it didn't take me long to discover that life insurance is where the profit is—both for the company and the agent. And within the life insurance market, selling whole-life insurance with a cash value is where you really make the big bucks. I soon

---

12. Proverbs 20:6.

caught on to what the insurance companies actually do. When you buy a whole-life policy, the company puts a term policy on you and invests the difference. That's what makes up a whole-life policy. (This is a bit oversimplified, but you get the idea of what happens.)

When I understood this, my conscience was uneasy. Either I could inform my clients that they could do the same thing—or I could be quiet and go along with the lucrative program.

Believe me, there is a lot of pressure that corporate America can place on an insurance agent to do things its way! Almost all the awards and trips offered by the insurance companies required a minimum amount of whole life to be sold. The devil tempted me to believe that I would not have to compromise my integrity in order to be successful.

Personal integrity—we all have to wrestle with it in different areas. Have you compromised yours? Is God speaking to your heart, your mind, your conscience, or your integrity right now? Are you brave enough to respond to His call? Do you have the courage to walk in your own integrity?

I just couldn't bring myself to follow corporate guidelines. I decided to sell term insurance instead. Yes, it cost me in the world's eyes, but my conscience was at rest and my clients were cared for.[13]

Even though I didn't acknowledge God at this time in my life, He was active in it, always calling me to take the higher road. When I look back over my life, it is amazing to me to see how God was there at every phase. Even while I was caught up in my mazes, He had His eye on me. His chisel was always at work to bring forth my integrity. To the extent that I cooperated with the process, His work in me went forward until that day I found myself standing before that dusty, narrow old door.

Back to that dusty, narrow old door

It wasn't actually a literal day. It was a period in my life in which my perception of God was changing from relating to Him as a distant theological concept to seeing Him as a real Person involved in my daily life.

After Sally and I sold everything, moved to our quaint log cabin in northwestern Montana, and started living on six thousand dollars a year, I experienced a real letdown.

I remember sitting out in the sandbox with my two young boys, playing "truckie." My brain was screaming, *What a waste of time!* I was bored to death and scared to death! I felt that life no longer had purpose. I didn't realize how much of my identity had been built around a bunch of plaques and achieve-

---

13. See Acts 24:16.

ment awards plastered on my wall, trips to Hawaii and Las Vegas, and diamond rings. I was used to running a business and cutting a profit and feeling like an important person. All of a sudden, it seemed that my life revolved around pushing trucks in the sandbox and going, *"Putt, putt, putt."*

In the midst of my deepening depression, that still, small Voice—that I now know to be God—whispered to my heart. *"Jim, I'm here. I have some things I want to teach you."* The sense that I was not alone, that God was with me and that He had a plan and a purpose even if I didn't, somehow soothed my fears and strengthened my fortitude.

You see, the simplicity and quietness of our wilderness home was already bringing me face-to-face with *the person I was not.* I wrestled with the hold that my temper had on me. My bias to irritation was as automatic as breathing. When I caught that whisper from God to my heart, I grabbed on to it like Jacob wrestling with the angel, and wouldn't let it go.

Up to this point, I knew God's promises in an external sort of way. Do you know what I'm talking about? I had read them. I could recite many of them. I could use them to lead you through an inspiring Bible study.

Now, I began to internalize them. I saw in them my lifeline to hope, to change, and to an authentic way of living. I saw that internalizing God's promises was my key to grasping God's presence. I lost that sense of His presence so easily. I could find it on my knees in the morning or before my open Bible, but when I entered my day, so often I found myself alone.

So I purchased a Bible the size of my back pocket. I carried that Bible with me everywhere I went. My boys used to wonder why I had it tucked under my arm while we cut firewood or why I had it open on the workbench while we tuned up our chainsaw. The reason was that I wanted to open it often, to touch it, and to be reminded of the presence of God behind those promises. Promises such as "I will never leave you nor forsake you." "No temptation has overtaken you except such as is common to man; but God is faithful, who will not allow you to be tempted beyond what you are able, but with the temptation will also make the way of escape, that you may be able to bear it."[14]

I wanted to keep those promises with me until I wouldn't lose that sense of God's presence in my life. When the Bible was near me, I could deal with the God of the Bible rather than being overwhelmed by the power that my flesh had over me.

As God's presence became more real to me, I began taking time-outs when God would tap me on my shoulder. Efficiency is my bugaboo. I can get so caught up in getting as many things done as quickly as possible that I become

---

14. Hebrews 13:5; 1 Corinthians 10:13.

very prone to anger or irritation when something gets in my way or doesn't go as I planned. At such times, God taps me on the shoulder (not literally, but by a prompting of my conscience) and reminds me, *"Slow down, Jim. You're headed for trouble."* This stage helped me understand that God was there and that I needed to tune in to Him.

I worked on this month after month after month. I would read God's Word and then try to apply it to that day's experience. I would go through hard times that left me begging God to remove the trial. Often, He wouldn't. But in time, I would see God's hand in it and know that He was still chiseling away at that block of stone that was me. My friends said I was nuts, but my wife started to see a different Jim Hohnberger.

Gradually, it started becoming clear to me that most people just have half of the Christian life. They either have the spirit or they have the truth. God wants us to experience and internalize both.[15]

As I continued forward in this daily process and I saw God come through for me time and time again—in the littlest things of life as well as the big ones— a confidence began to grow in me that the little boy under the teacher's desk had not had. God became very real and personal to me. I became quite content to be a nobody in the wilderness with my God, my wife, and my boys. But God had other plans.

I was invited to share my experience with a small group in Chicago. Then a Methodist university asked me to hold a weekend seminar. (The seminar was on wilderness survival, but the survival techniques I spoke about were quite different than what they were expecting. I brought God into the equation.)

From there, God continued to shape my experience, building on my time in the sandbox. He gave me a pulpit from which I share about how to find freedom in Him to thousands of people around the world. But God is not done sculpting Jim Hohnberger. The work continues, and only God sees what the final product will be.

But, by His grace, I will continue to cooperate with His chiseling. You see, I have caught the vision for my life in six simple words: *I will walk in my integrity.* And what is that integrity for Jim Hohnberger? It is rooted, grounded, and defined in God! He is the sieve I run everything through! He is the mandate for every undertaking! He is the perception that controls my reality! He is my North Star, my guiding Light, my Safety Net, and my Home Plate!

God is calling you to be the person you were born to be! No, you are not a Jimmy Hohnberger. You might not end up working in the pulpit. You might be an Elizabeth, raising a John the Baptist. You might be like the demoniac

---

15. See John 4:23, 24.

Jesus sent home to share with his friends and neighbors what great things God had done for him. You might be that edelweiss flower that blooms out its little heart on an eight-thousand-foot-high mountain ledge, where the only eye that sees and acknowledges its beauty is the eye of God. But the sculpture of your life needs to take shape. Embrace the process. Walk in your integrity!

God is calling to you as you plod on life's treadmill through your various mazes. He's knocking on that dusty, narrow old door in your heart and mine. The devil doesn't want us to answer that call. He piles up all kinds of obstacles, hoping we will become discouraged from finding our real destiny. Other voices clamor for our attention—our career, our recreation, our peers, or our past— even our misperceptions of Him. Many brush His call aside as irrelevant and continue to madly chase after their mirages. Others pause to gaze thoughtfully at the door, but fear to venture further. Some begin the journey, but then tire of the protracted effort involved and return to the familiar ruts of life. A few enter through the door and pursue it with all their hearts.[16]

God is calling, "Come, walk with Me!" What will you do?

Questions to ponder or discuss with others:

1. Do you relate to Mahana?
2. In what ways are you hiding under the teacher's desk?
3. Do you fit in too well with your peers?
4. Does peer pressure cause your "belonging" to compromise your calling?
5. Do you know what it means to walk in your own integrity?
6. Would others say you possess a personal integrity?
7. Is God calling you to take some "Enoch time"?
8. Do you know how to listen to God?
9. Are you sailing your own seas?
10. Have you dared to own your own life?
11. Are you cooperating with God's chiseling process?
12. Will you step through that dusty, narrow old door and walk in your integrity?

---

16. See Matthew 7:13, 14.

Want to Know MORE About the Hohnbergers?

E mpowered Living Ministries is the outgrowth of Jim and Sally's experience with God. Located near Glacier National Park, the ministry office is here to serve your needs, whether it is to book a speaking engagement, request a media appearance, or order any of a large variety of resource materials, including books, booklets, and seminars on CD or DVD. For more information, contact:

Empowered Living Ministries
3945 North Fork Road
Columbia Falls, MT 59912

EMPOWEREDLIVINGMINISTRIES.ORG

Phone 406-387-4333
Orders 877-755-8300
Fax 406-387-4336